TEEN GUIDE TO HEALTH

How to Be Your Best Self: Physical, Emotional & Social

For information regarding permission,
Contact us:
www.reachoutrecovery.com

ISBN: 978-1-7324158-5-0

Printed in the U.S.A.
First Printing, August 2019
1 2 3 4 5 6 7 8 9 10

Book Design
Haley LaFerney

Research and Editorial
Leslie Glass
Samantha Curreli

TEEN GUIDE TO HEALTH

How to Be Your Best Self: Physical, Emotional & Social

TABLE OF CONTENTS

INTRODUCTION

Why is this teen health guide different from any other? Teens need a simple primer for understanding their body, brain, and emotional health. When working with high school and college students over the last decade, we have observed that basic knowledge about health, mental health, and wellness is lacking. Teens feel sadness and despair, and too many young people don't have crucial life skills. Mental health is not widely understood, and teens fear being seen as not normal. Without a clear understanding and acceptance of human differences, no one feels truly mentally healthy. It's that simple.

Teens may look good and perform well on tests and still not be emotionally or physically healthy. And even when they are, they may not think so. Further, when students are unhappy or unsafe at home, they are at even greater risk for depression, self harm, and other unhealthy or risky behaviors.

Our most precious resources simply don't know how to express their emotional needs and protect themselves. This lack of knowledge puts them at risk for substance experimentation when their brains aren't fully developed which too often leads to adverse experiences with lasting negative impact. We wanted to create a basic, relatable overview that explains how physical, emotional and social life are all connected and the ways that substances impact the body, brain, and emotional health. Knowing how to be healthy is the first step to getting healthy. This guide does not include information about many substances which can be found in the Teen Guide to Health: Alcohol and Substances Supplement.

CHAPTER ONE

GOOD HEALTH IS NOT JUST PHYSICAL

People come in all shapes, sizes, colors, and ages. That is the beauty of humanity. We're not just one kind of person. Humans may be one species, but there are millions of varieties. No matter where you are, being healthy is more than physical, and people have different needs at every age. To make health even more complicated, each culture has its own beliefs, ideals and rules: What you can do and can't do. What you should and shouldn't look like. How you should act. What if you live in a culture that doesn't value who you are and the special qualities you have? This is where emotional health plays a big part in how healthy and successful you can be.

Health has three components:
Physical, emotional, and social, and they are all connected. They all contribute to mental health. Your body and brain work together to make you who you are, and to influence the kind of relationships you have. Your relationships help determine how well you can learn and flourish. Every culture tends to value people based on their physical beauty or prowess, their intelligence and brainpower. Even more important, however, are qualities and influences we can't see. Creativity, resilience, pain, loneliness, low self-esteem, damage from dysfunctional families.

WHAT 3 COMPONENTS
MAKE YOU HEALTHY?

HOW CAN CULTURE
IMPACT GOOD HEALTH?

WHAT QUALITIES
CAN'T WE SEE?

You can't see people's emotional IQ from the outside, but all these things affect you and can be barriers to your health and success.

NOBODY IS PERFECT

There is no such thing as a totally normal child, teen, or adult. Not one of us has every component related to good health. Do you know anyone who is totally confident, super smart, has wonderful eating and sleeping habits, great relationships, and a wonderfully supportive, sober family? Oh, and this imaginary person is talented and has a perfect body, too. Exactly. No one, and no family is perfect. Everywhere you look you can see people of all ages struggling with some aspect of their personality, work, relationships, or physical life.

WHAT KEEPS YOU HEALTHY

There are many components to good health. Our bodies are just one part of being healthy. Not having perfect health in your body, however, doesn't mean you can't be healthy in many other ways. Is this a new idea? We humans are subject to many physical diseases. Diabetes, heart disease, blood diseases, and cancer are just a few illnesses that need treatment and management over a lifetime. All kinds of physical and mental disabilities need special treatment and care. Trauma from poverty, war, or abuse requires understanding, love, and support.

Brain diseases, mental illness, and recovery from a substance or behavior disorders are also common illnesses that require treatment, ongoing care, and management over a lifetime. It's okay. Physical and mental illnesses are part of being human. Emotional and behavioral health are equally important to having good health. Being unhealthy emotionally impacts your physical health just as your physical health can affect your emotions. Every aspect of you works with other aspects of you. You might think of us as suitcases which contain our bodies, emotions, and behaviors. We can't change our physical body systems, but we can rearrange and adjust emotional and social elements of our lives to grow and flourish.

PEOPLE ARE DIFFERENT & THE SAME

Some people are healthier than others physically. Some people are well adjusted; others have difficulty expressing themselves and making good decisions. Many students have experienced trauma and emotional or physical abuse that make expressing themselves and trusting people difficult. Families face all kinds of crises and stress at different times. No life is perfect from childhood to old age. Parents get divorced and remarry. Financial problems cause stress. Siblings can be engaged in risky behaviors or substance use. Family members pass away. These, and many other factors outside our control, affect our emotional life and our behavior. They are called Adverse Childhood Experiences. Adverse experiences happen at every age. Pandemics, poverty, war, and political strife are all examples of adverse experiences that hurt everyone.

We can't say it often enough. No one is perfect. No one has it all. No life is all happiness. The beauty of humanity is that each one of us is different. We look different from each other, have different skills, think differently about issues, communicate in different ways and have really different lifestyles. But as different as we all are in so many ways, we all need the exactly the same things to have good health. What are the four factors that keep us healthy and balanced?

CHAPTER TWO
PHYSICAL HEALTH

In the simplest and narrowest terms, physical health
is the starting point of a balanced and healthy life.
The five most basic needs for physical health include:
Sleeping enough every day to recharge your brain and
body and balance your emotions. Eating a nutritious
diet to fuel your brain and body. Showering, washing
your face and hands and cleaning your teeth every day
for good hygiene. Exercising to develop, or maintain,
good physical condition. Avoiding substances and
alcohol that affect organ and brain functions and all
the behaviors needed for a productive life.

5 Physical Health Components

Getting enough rest (sleep)

Good Nutrition (food)

Hygiene (keeping ourselves neat and clean)

Exercise (get moving)

Staying Drug Free

WHY DOES BEING
DRUG FREE MATTER?

WHY DO SLEEP AND
DIET MATTER?

WHY DOES EXERCISE
MATTER?

Chapter Two Physical Health

GETTING ENOUGH REST

Did you know that teens need more sleep than adults, around 9 hours every day? Why do teens need that much sleep? Sleep is fuel for the brain and helps control emotions. Not getting enough sleep causes moodiness, lack of alertness, and concentration problems.

TIPS FOR GOOD SLEEP HYGIENE

1. Get up at the same time every day to regulate sleep rhythms. Sleep only an hour or two longer on weekends.

2. Take naps when possible. Sleep experts recommend midday naps and other short bursts of sleep. In fact, studies show that deep sleep can help us function optimally, even if it's just a half-hour nap. Nap time is just a wish for most teens.

3. Unplug earlier. Smartphones keep you awake and alert. Even worse, they emit more artificial light than the sun itself. Light stimulates more cortisol, the hormone that tells the brain to be alert and productive.

4. Exercise. Research shows that people sleep better and feel more alert during the day if they get at least 150 minutes of exercise a week.

5. Avoid sugar at night. Sugar destabilizes our glucose levels, creating a burst of energy. That's followed by a drop in blood sugar that, in turn, stimulates the release of adrenaline and cortisol – waking us up in the wee hours.

GOOD NUTRITION

What kinds of food do you need for your body to function well? What kinds of food does your brain need to develop? How much food is too little or too much? Eating disorders are common among teens in many cultures. One sign of an eating disorder is feeling guilty or anxious around food. There are other reasons people are anxious around food. Allergies to foods can be one reason. Another might be food insecurity. An eating disorder, however, is when people are compelled to eat whether hungry or not, or not to eat even when starving. People with food disorders will hide the problem from others, fearing their loved ones and friends won't approve.

Whenever you have to hide what you're doing, it's a sign that you might be doing something that can hurt you. Eating disorders which involve eating too much or too little, affect your brain, body chemistry, weight, and emotional wellbeing.

Feeling anxious or worried around food is natural, however, for people who are food insecure. When you don't know where your next meal is coming from or whether you are going to have enough to eat, anxiety around food is both normal and may stay with you in adulthood. This kind of worry or guilt about food is trauma related.

4 NUTRITION QUESTIONS TO ASK YOURSELF

1. Do you eat foods that give you energy, or foods that send you on a roller coaster of ups and downs?

2. Do you drink enough water?

3. Do you eat what's closest at hand instead of what's healthiest?

4. Do you grab fast food that tastes great but is full of sugar, empty carbs and fat?

COMPONENTS OF A HEALTHY DIET

Vegetables: dark green, red and orange, legumes (beans and peas), starchy and other vegetables.

Fruits: especially fresh whole fruit.

Grains: at least half of which are whole grain.

Dairy: low-fat milk, yogurt, cheese, and/or fortified soy beverages.

Proteins: seafood, lean meats and poultry, eggs, legumes (beans and peas), soy products, and nuts and seeds.

Oils, including those from plants: canola, corn, olive, peanut, safflower, soybean, and sunflower. Oils also are naturally present in nuts, seeds, seafood, olives, and avocados.

FOOD CAN GIVE YOU ENERGY OR SLOW YOU DOWN

What you eat and how much or little you eat affects your physical health in more ways than one. Our eating habits often depend on the culture of our family and the kind of foods we get at home. Every culture has its favorite foods and style of eating. Healthy eating may be a family commitment or a new idea.

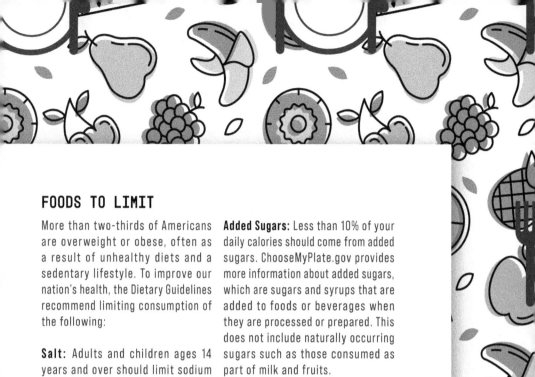

FOODS TO LIMIT

More than two-thirds of Americans are overweight or obese, often as a result of unhealthy diets and a sedentary lifestyle. To improve our nation's health, the Dietary Guidelines recommend limiting consumption of the following:

Salt: Adults and children ages 14 years and over should limit sodium to less than 2,300 mg per day, and children younger than 14 years should consume even less. Use the Nutrition Facts label to check for sodium, especially in processed foods like pizza, pasta dishes, sauces, and soups.

Saturated and Trans Fats: Less than 10% of your daily calories should come from saturated fats. Foods that are high in saturated fat include butter, whole milk, meats that are not labeled as lean, and tropical oils such as coconut and palm oil. Saturated fats should be replaced with unsaturated fats, such as canola or olive oil.

Added Sugars: Less than 10% of your daily calories should come from added sugars. ChooseMyPlate.gov provides more information about added sugars, which are sugars and syrups that are added to foods or beverages when they are processed or prepared. This does not include naturally occurring sugars such as those consumed as part of milk and fruits.

HYGIENE

Hygiene means the art of health. Personal hygiene habits include: Washing your hands and brushing and flossing your teeth to keep away bacteria, viruses, and illnesses. There are mental as well as physical benefits to good grooming. Practicing good body hygiene helps you feel good about yourself, which is important for your mental health.

POOR HYGIENE HINTS AT HEALTH ISSUES

If people you know haven't bathed or appear unkempt, it could be a sign that they are depressed. When people are sad or depressed, they neglect themselves. This also occurs when people use drugs and alcohol. People who have poor hygiene — dirty hair and clothes, body odor, bad breath, missing teeth, and the like — often are seen as unhealthy and may face discrimination. On the other hand, people who practice good grooming in addition to personal hygiene have greater self-esteem and emotional

health. Good grooming includes keeping your clothes tidy and clean, caring about what you wear and how you look, and tending to your hair and face.

5 BASIC HYGIENE TIPS

1. Bathe Regularly Wash your body every day. Shampoo your hair often. Your body is constantly shedding skin that needs to come off. Otherwise, it can cause illnesses. Your scalp needs the same kind of attention. Shampoo your hair frequently.

2. Trim Your Nails Keeping your finger and toenails trimmed and in good shape will prevent problems such as hangnails and infected nail beds. Feet that are clean and dry are less likely to contract athlete's foot.

3. Brush And Floss Your Teeth Ideally, you should brush your teeth after every meal. At the very least, brush your teeth twice a day and floss daily. Brushing minimizes the accumulation of bacteria in your mouth, which can cause tooth decay and gum disease.

Flossing, too, helps maintain strong, healthy gums. The bacteria that builds up and causes gum disease can go straight to the heart and cause very serious valve problems. Unhealthy gums also can cause your teeth to loosen, which makes it difficult to chew and to eat properly. To maintain a healthy smile, visit the dentist for checkups and cleanings.

4. Wash Your Hands Washing your hands often is more important than ever before. Be sure to wash your hands before preparing or eating food, going to the bathroom, coughing or sneezing and after handling garbage. That goes a long way toward preventing the spread of bacteria and viruses. And don't touch your face.

5. Sleep Tight Get plenty of rest — 8 to 10 hours a night — so that you are refreshed and are ready to take on the day every morning. Lack of sleep can leave you feeling run down and can compromise your body's natural defenses, your immune system.

EXERCISE

When people are physically fit, they feel and look better. All the health statistics show the positive results of moving and getting fit. Let's face it, not everyone loves the idea of running around, mastering a sport, working up a sweat, and being physically active. If your parents aren't fans of fitness, or are sports spectators only, you may not have the exercise habit.

Exercise is a natural high, and an important part of daily living. In countries where kids have to walk miles to school or live in rural areas where they work on farms, getting enough exercise is no problem. Their daily routines include plenty of exercise and outdoor time. For kids who live in cities and travel by school bus or car, exercise may not seem like a necessity. Yet, it is every bit as important as getting enough sleep, eating the right foods and regular hygiene.

10 BENEFITS OF EXERCISE

1. Strengthens The Heart The heart is a muscle. Like other muscles, your heart's performance improves when it's regularly challenged. The heart responds to exercise by becoming stronger and more efficient. Strengthening the heart muscle can help ward off heart disease even in early childhood. Heart disease is the leading cause of death for those who have poor diets and don't exercise.

2. Keeps Arteries And Veins Clear Exercise reduces the amount of harmful cholesterol and fats in a person's blood. It increases the flexibility of the walls of blood vessels and helps to lower blood pressure. This can reduce a person's risk for heart attack and stroke.

3. Strengthens the Lungs Working hard increases lung capacity, and their efficiency in moving air in and out of the body. As a result, more oxygen is drawn into the body and

more carbon dioxide and other waste gases are expelled. Regular exercise helps prevent the decline in oxygen intake that occurs naturally with age or as a result of inactivity.

4. Reduces Blood Sugar Levels Exercise prevents sugar from accumulating in the blood by triggering muscles to take up more glucose from the bloodstream and use it for energy. This can reduce a person's risk of developing diabetes.

5. Controls Weight When people are sedentary, they tend to take in more calories than necessary. These unused calories accumulate as fat. People who are physically active may have a deficit of calories, which takes fat away and lowers weight. Lowered weight is good for the heart and can be beneficial in people with diabetes.

6. Strengthens Bones Just as muscles grow stronger when physically stressed, bones also respond by getting stronger. Exercise increases Bone Density, which helps prevent osteoporosis, a condition in which bones lose density, weaken, and become porous and fragile.

7. Helps Prevent Cancer People who exercise regularly have lower incidences of cancer. The cancers most affected include colon, prostate, uterine, and breast cancers.

8. Regulates Blood Pressure Exercise has been shown to reduce stress levels. As the levels of stress in a person's body subsides, blood pressure and risk for heart disease decline.

9. Improves Energy Levels Regular exercise often makes people feel more energetic, allows them to be more active, and reduces the likelihood that they'll tire during the day.

10. Enhances Emotional Wellbeing Most people report that they feel calm and have a sense of well-being after they exercise. Exercise, according to one theory, releases beta-endorphin, a natural substance in the body that is hundreds of times more potent than morphine. Another theory points to serotonin as the cause of the exercise high. Increased levels of serotonin in the central nervous system are associated with feelings of well-being, heightening of appetite, and lessening of mental depression. The weight loss that accompanies exercise can also cause people to feel better about themselves.

STAYING DRUG FREE

Staying drug free protects your brain and keeps you safe at school. You may be curious about substances and alcohol. If you have siblings who drink or use drugs you may be encouraged to try. Some of your peers are experimenting and seem to be having fun. The opposite is the truth. In fact, 15% of all teens get into trouble because of drugs or alcohol. That means they're having problems at school and at home. The problems related to substance use get worse over time without treatment. Here's the reason. Drugs affect the teen brain. It's a fact. You may think you're fully developed already because your hormones tell you so, and you look grown up. But your brain hasn't finished developing yet and will continue to develop for many years, until you are 26. Substance use can actually halt crucial brain development.

WHY IS IT IMPORTANT TO BE DRUG FREE

In the coming chapters, you will learn what happens to your body when you experiment with medicines that are not prescribed for you as well as substances that can hurt, and even kill you. Substances, including tobacco, vaping, marijuana, alcohol, and illegal drugs affect your brain and body in ways that may surprise you. Substances and alcohol can hurt you today, but can also have a lasting impact on your brain and your ability to learn, be healthy, and to grow. Ties between substance use and mental health problems are strong. Teens who experiment with drugs, tobacco, and alcohol are more likely to develop full-blown addictions either as teens or later as adults.

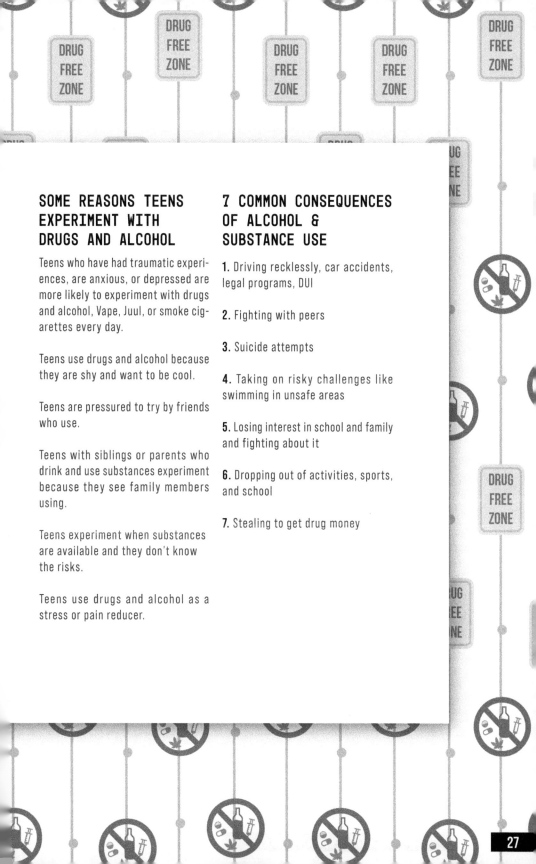

SOME REASONS TEENS EXPERIMENT WITH DRUGS AND ALCOHOL

Teens who have had traumatic experiences, are anxious, or depressed are more likely to experiment with drugs and alcohol, Vape, Juul, or smoke cigarettes every day.

Teens use drugs and alcohol because they are shy and want to be cool.

Teens are pressured to try by friends who use.

Teens with siblings or parents who drink and use substances experiment because they see family members using.

Teens experiment when substances are available and they don't know the risks.

Teens use drugs and alcohol as a stress or pain reducer.

7 COMMON CONSEQUENCES OF ALCOHOL & SUBSTANCE USE

1. Driving recklessly, car accidents, legal programs, DUI

2. Fighting with peers

3. Suicide attempts

4. Taking on risky challenges like swimming in unsafe areas

5. Losing interest in school and family and fighting about it

6. Dropping out of activities, sports, and school

7. Stealing to get drug money

" NIDA'S TOP 10 QUESTIONS TEENS ASK ABOUT DRUGS

1.Why do people take drugs when they know they're bad Every day we make choices that affect our health. People take drugs for a lot of different reasons, like to deal with life's challenges, to escape from reality, to relieve pain, or to try to fit in—just to name a few.

Some people can be aware of the negative effects of drugs on their health and in their life and still struggle to stop using them. This is because repeated drug use can lead to changes in the brain that make it hard to stop using them, even when people want to stop. When this happens, the person is experiencing a medical problem known as substance use disorder. Addiction is a severe form of substance use disorder.

All addictive drugs cause the brain to release the chemical dopamine. Dopamine is usually released after pleasurable and satisfying activities. Dopamine causes the brain to remember rewards, like food and sex, and reinforces the desire to seek them out again. Repeatedly using a drug floods the brain with more dopamine, which can change the way the brain responds to that drug.

With repeated use, a greater quantity of drug is needed to produce the same pleasurable effect. When the drug is not available, people may experience the negative symptoms of withdrawal, which may include stress, anxiety, depression, and sometimes physical symptoms such as sweating, vomiting and pain. Repeated cycles of drug use and withdrawal can disrupt brain function to the extent that people may have difficultly experiencing pleasure in their daily lives. At this point, many people continue drug use to avoid the lows caused by withdrawal rather than seek the highs they once experienced.

Fortunately, treatment can help people with a substance use disorder counteract these disruptive effects and lead healthier lives. The sooner a person receives treatment, the better the chance that they will recover.

2.What are the effects of drugs like Xanax & Percocet Xanax® and Percocet® are both brand names of prescription drugs. Both can help treat certain medical conditions when used as directed by a doctor, but they have the potential to be misused.

They work in the brain in different ways: Xanax®, or alprazolam, is a prescription depressant to help people with anxiety. Percocet® is prescribed to treat severe pain from serious injuries or after surgery. It contains the analgesics (pain relievers) acetaminophen (the same drug as in Tylenol®) and oxycodone, which is an opioid.

Xanax® and Percocet® can cause severe adverse health effects, including overdose, if taken in large quantities or if taken with certain other drugs. Large doses of acetaminophen in Percocet® can also cause life-threatening liver damage.

3.What are bath salts When teens ask us about bath salts, we understand that they're probably not referring to Epsom salt for a relaxing time in the tub. They're talking about synthetic cathinones, which are stimulants made in labs. Bath salts and similar drugs cause extreme wakefulness and elevated heart and breathing rates. Many people seek out these drugs because they are viewed as a cheaper substitute for stimulants like methamphetamine and cocaine.

Using bath salts can cause severe intoxication, hallucinations, paranoia, panic attacks, and addiction. Serious health effects including dehydration and kidney problems can also occur. An additional danger of taking these synthetic drugs is that they might contain other substances with their own harmful effects, including life-threatening overdoses.

4.Can you get addicted to ADHD meds Many teens who have been diagnosed with attention-deficit/hyperactivity disorder (ADHD) take prescription stimulants like Adderall® or Ritalin® to help treat their symptoms. When taken as directed, these medications can be helpful and safe, and have a very low risk for addiction. If your doctor prescribes stimulants, it's important to follow the instructions and to discuss any concerns about addiction or dependence.

Sometimes people who don't have ADHD take drugs like Adderall® or Ritalin® in an attempt to get high, to stay awake longer, or to stay focused while studying. According to the Monitoring the Future annual survey on teen drug use, there was a significant increase in the misuse of the ADHD medicine Adderall® among 8th graders from 2015 to 2020.

This can be especially harmful because people often take these medications at a higher dose or through a different route than prescribed. Misusing ADHD medications can cause headaches, nausea, feeling anxious, and sleeping problems. Misusing prescription stimulants can also lead to addiction. These drugs can also make you feel paranoid, cause your body temperature to get dangerously high, and make your heartbeat too fast. While stimulants may help with a lack of focus in some people, they may diminish other skills (like creative thinking).

5.Is vaping bad for you even if it's just flavoring Research shows that many teens and young adults don't realize that the flavors they use actually can contain nicotine, an addictive compound found in tobacco. Many vapes also contain propylene glycol, glycerin, chemical flavorings, and other compounds with unknown health effects. As a result, people who vape—even just flavoring—may inhale and ingest potentially harmful chemicals.

Recent studies showed that students who had already used any type of e-cigarette by the time they started 9th grade were more likely than others to start smoking cigarettes and other smokable tobacco products within the next year. And we know that cigarette smoking is a leading cause of cancer and other illnesses. According to the Centers for Disease Control and Prevention (CDC), cigarettes cause more than 480,000 premature deaths in the United States each year—from smoking or exposure to secondhand smoke. This represents about 1 in every 5 U.S. deaths, or 1,300 deaths every day.

Other vaping products can also cause harm. In 2020, thousands of people got sick and dozens died from an illness called EVALI, which stands for e-cigarette or vaping-use associated lung injury. Vitamin E acetate, an additive in some THC-containing vaping products, is strongly linked to EVALI. When heated and inhaled, vitamin E acetate can damage the lungs.

6.How can I help someone with a problem stop taking drugs & How can I help if they don't want help Asking how to help someone who may have a substance use disorder to stop taking drugs is one of the most common things we hear from both adults and teens. Fortunately, there are resources to help people affected by a friend or family member's substance use or substance use disorder.

NIDA's Step-by-Step Guides have resources and information on how to recognize a substance use disorder and how to find help. NIDA for Teens has additional resources to find help for teens.

Supporting a loved one through a struggle with substance use can be difficult for adults and teens alike. This process can be especially complicated when someone is resistant to getting help. While you may not have control over someone else's substance use, support is available to cope with how that substance use may affect you.

7.If a pregnant woman takes drugs/ smokes/drinks alcohol, what happens to her baby Pregnancy is an important time to maintain or adopt healthy behaviors. Decades of research show exposure to certain substances can be unsafe for the health of the woman and the baby. Many drugs, including opioids, alcohol, and stimulants, have been associated with harm to the developing fetus. Using or being exposed to some substances can increase the risk of miscarriage and can cause migraines, seizures, or high blood pressure in the mother. A 2013 study found the risk of stillbirth was 2 to 3 times greater in women whose blood tests showed exposure to tobacco and about 2 times greater in women whose blood tests showed exposure to cannabis, stimulants, or prescription pain relievers. Pregnant women should refrain from drinking alcohol and talk with their health care provider before using any medicines or drugs.

8.Can marijuana be used as medicine Although the medical use of marijuana is legal in many states, the U.S. Food and Drug Administration (FDA) has not determined that the marijuana plant is safe and effective for treating any disease or condition and has not approved it as a medicine.

Although the marijuana plant has not been approved as medicine, the FDA has approved formulations of two of the components of marijuana—THC and CBD—as medicine for specific conditions. THC, which stands for delta-9-tetrahydrocannabinol, is responsible for marijuana's "high", the euphoric and addictive effects of the drug. CBD, or cannabidiol, does not produce a high and has not been shown to lead to addiction.

CBD derived from the marijuana plant has been approved seizures associated with specific disorders, and laboratory-made THC has been approved to help with appetite in people with AIDS and to treat nausea associated with chemotherapy for people with cancer. Although not available in the United States, a combination of plant-derived THC and CBD has been approved in multiple countries to treat some symptoms of multiple sclerosis.

9.Which is more habit forming - smoking cigarettes or vaping nicotine Nicotine in any form is highly addictive, and many who start using one form of nicotine transition to another.

NIDA's 2020 Monitoring the Future survey showed that the number of teens who say they vape nicotine has leveled off but remains high. The number of teens who say they smoked cigarettes in the past month declined significantly since the mid-1990s and is now at or near the lowest it ever has been. Because both smoking and vaping are so addictive, it is helpful to speak with a doctor when trying to quit either. A good strategy is never to start.

10.What is the worst drug It's only natural to want to know what's best or worst, good or bad. That's why we love these types of lists! But in the case of drugs and alcohol, there isn't a "worst" just as there isn't a "best" drug.

We don't define drugs as most or least harmful. All drugs have the potential to produce negative health effects or lead to a dangerous situation in the short or long term. Whether a drug causes a serious health issue—like a life-threatening overdose—can depend on how much a person uses, how they consume it, and other factors.

However, some drugs are so potent that a life-threatening overdose can occur the first time a person uses them. For example, the synthetic opioid fentanyl is 100 times more potent than morphine and 50 times more potent than heroin. Because fentanyl is often mixed with other drugs, such as heroin, cocaine, methamphetamine, and MDMA (Molly), fentanyl may be ingested unknowingly at unknown quantities, which can lead to overdose. Injecting potent drugs can be particularly dangerous because this route delivers the compounds more directly to the brain than ingesting or snorting drugs. Injection also carries the risks of injury and infection.

Similarly, some drugs are more frequently associated with addiction and dependence than others. For example, more than half of people who regularly use cigarettes meet the criteria for a tobacco use disorder, while only about 1 in 11 people who regularly use marijuana (cannabis) meet the criteria for a cannabis use disorder. Certain drugs can have a stronger effect on the brain than others. Research has shown that methamphetamine, in particular, may damage cells and structures within the brain that can cause long-term problems with emotion and memory.

Certain physical or mental illnesses, as well as family health history, also influence someone's chances of developing an addiction or other negative health effects of drug use. Age is an especially important factor when calculating the risks of substance use. Because the brain develops through a person's mid-twenties, teens and young adults tend to be more vulnerable to negative health effects of many drugs. All of this means certain substances may pose different risks to different people in different situations.

Going by the numbers, determining the deadliest drug also depends on perspective.

In 2021 more than 100,000 people died from a drug-involved overdose in the United States. The most common drugs associated with these fatal overdoses were synthetic opioids, including the highly potent synthetic opioid fentanyl.

However, the long-term health effects of cigarette smoking are responsible for more than 480,000 deaths per year. That's about 1,300 deaths every day.

And alcohol is the substance most frequently involved in deadly car crashes. Nearly one person died every 52 minutes from drunk driving crashes in 2019.

To put it simply, what's the "worst" drug isn't an easy question to answer, and it's important to understand the risks of any substance. NIDA supports research to help us understand the effect of drugs on the brain, how to prevent people from starting to use drugs, and how to help them if they have substance use disorder. And NIDA for Teens has resources available to help teens learn about specific substances, mental health, and their growing brains.

SOURCE : National Institute on Drug Abuse; National Institutes of Health; U.S. Department of Health and Human Services.

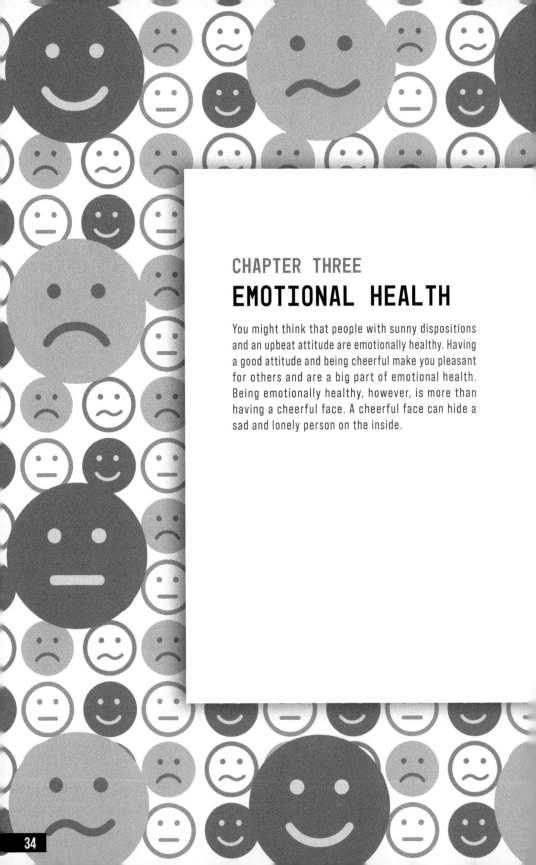

CHAPTER THREE
EMOTIONAL HEALTH

You might think that people with sunny dispositions and an upbeat attitude are emotionally healthy. Having a good attitude and being cheerful make you pleasant for others and are a big part of emotional health. Being emotionally healthy, however, is more than having a cheerful face. A cheerful face can hide a sad and lonely person on the inside.

For our purposes there are five components that define Emotional Health.

Expressing yourself in an appropriate way

Managing your emotions and feelings

Coping well with stress

Making good decisions

Solving problems

HOW ARE YOU
FEELING INSIDE?

HOW DO YOU EXPRESS
YOUR EMOTIONS?

HOW DO YOU
MANAGE STRESS?

CAN YOU FIGURE OUT
WHAT TO DO WHEN YOU
HAVE PROBLEMS?

What are the signs of an emotionally healthy person ?

Learning to be in control of thoughts, feelings, and behaviors is an essential part of growing up. Toddlers need to be taught what they can and can't do so they don't run wild and hurt themselves. It's the same with all the facets of your emotional health. Sometimes it is hard to know what's right and what you should do. You may wonder if the feelings you are experiencing are serious depression or the kind of sadness, worry and anxiety we all feel from time to time no matter how healthy we are. You may experience many different feelings during just one day. How can you balance your emotions when you're not even sure what's happening inside?

UNDERSTANTING YOUR EMOTIONS TO GET HELP WHEN YOU NEED IT

You may have been hurt by someone, or something, and can't make the abuse stop. Or, you may not be able to get over a hurtful or painful event only you know about. You may live in a family that says everything is okay when you know everything isn't okay at all. You may have family members who don't allow you to ask questions or seek help. You may have a bully you can't expose. Many people grow up without the freedom to talk about feelings. Being able to identify and express your feelings is very important for emotional health. The first step to emotional health is being free to tell someone what's going on inside you to help you understand and manage your thoughts and behavior. If there is no one in your immediate family for you to confide in, there might be an aunt or a teacher who is safe to talk to.

DOES EMOTIONAL HEALTH HAVE TO BE NURTURED

If the components of emotional health came naturally, we would all be able to cope with stress and challenges, know the right things to do and say, and be able to accomplish everything expected of us with no problem. We'd see everything in perspective. We'd bounce back when we're hurt or experience failure. We'd be able to remain stable no matter what crises our families face. This isn't the case. We learn emotional health through our experiences, and with the help of family, friends, teachers, coaches, mentors, therapists, and others to whom we can turn for guidance and support. There are many people, not just family members, who can help and guide us to emotional health.

"

5 COMPONENTS OF
EMOTIONAL INTELLIGENCE

SELF-AWARENESS

If you're self-aware, you can see your own patterns of behaviors and motives. You know how your emotions and actions impact those around you, for better or for worse. You can name your own emotions when they come up and understand why they're there.

You can also recognize your triggers, identify your strengths, and see your own limitations.

Being self-aware can also mean you're humble—we're all only human, after all.

SELF-REGULATION

If you can self-regulate, your emotional reactions are in proportion to the given circumstances.

You know how to pause, as needed, and control your impulses. You think before you act and consider the consequences.

It also means you know how to ease tension, manage conflict, cope with difficult scenarios, and adapt to changes in your environment. It's all about bringing out the part of yourself that helps manage emotions.

MOTIVATION

If you're intrinsically motivated, you have a thirst for personal development. You're highly driven to succeed, whatever your version of success looks like.

You're inspired to accomplish goals because it helps you grow as a person, rather than doing it for outside rewards like money, fame, status, or recognition.

EMPATHY

If you're empathic, you're at a healthy level of self-interested — but not self-centered.

In conversations, you can understand where someone is coming from. You can "walk a mile in their shoes," so to speak. Even if the exact scenario hasn't happened to you, you can draw on your life experience to imagine how it may feel and be compassionate about what they're going through.

You're slow to judge others and possess the awareness that we're all just doing the best we can with the circumstances we've been given. When we know better, we do better.

SOCIAL SKILLS

If you've developed your social skills, you're adept at working in teams. You're aware of others and their needs in a conversation or conflict resolution.

You're welcoming in conversation, using active listening, eye contact, verbal communication skills, and open body language. You know how to develop a rapport with others or express leadership, if the occasion calls for it.

WHY IS EMOTIONAL INTELLIGENCE IMPORTANT

Humans are social animals — we're wired for connection. The more we can build positive relationships and develop cooperative connections, the more enriching our lives may be.

The term "emotional intelligence" was coined in the 1990s, then popularized by psychologist and author Daniel Goleman in his book "Emotional Intelligence: Why It Can Matter More Than IQ."

SOURCE: PsychCentral

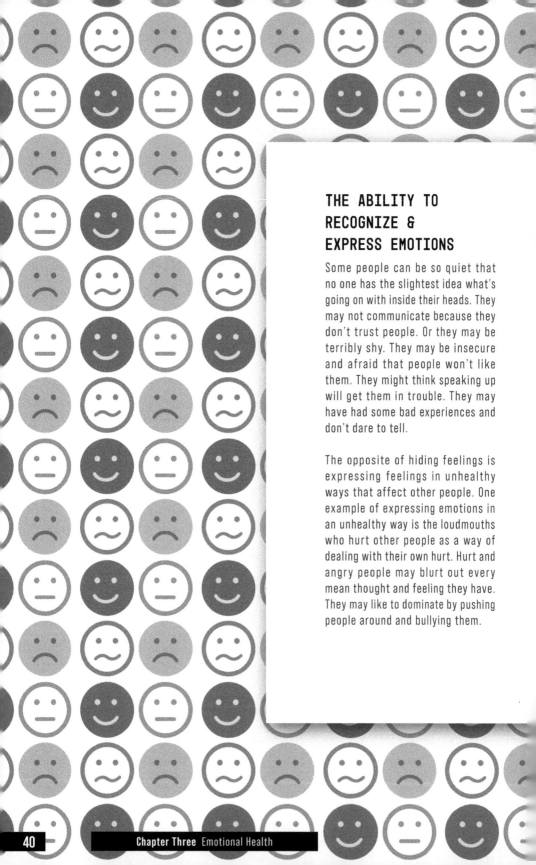

THE ABILITY TO RECOGNIZE & EXPRESS EMOTIONS

Some people can be so quiet that no one has the slightest idea what's going on with inside their heads. They may not communicate because they don't trust people. Or they may be terribly shy. They may be insecure and afraid that people won't like them. They might think speaking up will get them in trouble. They may have had some bad experiences and don't dare to tell.

The opposite of hiding feelings is expressing feelings in unhealthy ways that affect other people. One example of expressing emotions in an unhealthy way is the loudmouths who hurt other people as a way of dealing with their own hurt. Hurt and angry people may blurt out every mean thought and feeling they have. They may like to dominate by pushing people around and bullying them.

Both acting out in angry ways and suppressing your true feelings are indications help is needed to express emotions in a healthy way. When you express yourself in a healthy way, you feel better and don't hurt others. What if you're deeply sad, or angry, or feel hurt? What if you've been told you're not smart or good looking and don't feel good enough? How do you share those feelings in a healthy way?

For those who are hurting, finding an adult to help can be the answer. Everyone needs safe people who can help them understand their thoughts and feelings. We'd all like to be validated and reassured we're good enough. But what if there isn't a safe adult near you? How can you understand your feelings and find ways to express yourself in healthy ways?

Positive self expression can have many forms. Shy and hurting people can express themselves through music, or art, or writing, or helping others. One kind of healthy self expression is journaling. Writing for a few minutes every day about whatever is happening in your life can help you identify your feelings and neutralize pain and frustration. One example might be writing notes or letters to people to tell them what you think, but not sending them. Journaling is a great tool for healthy expression.

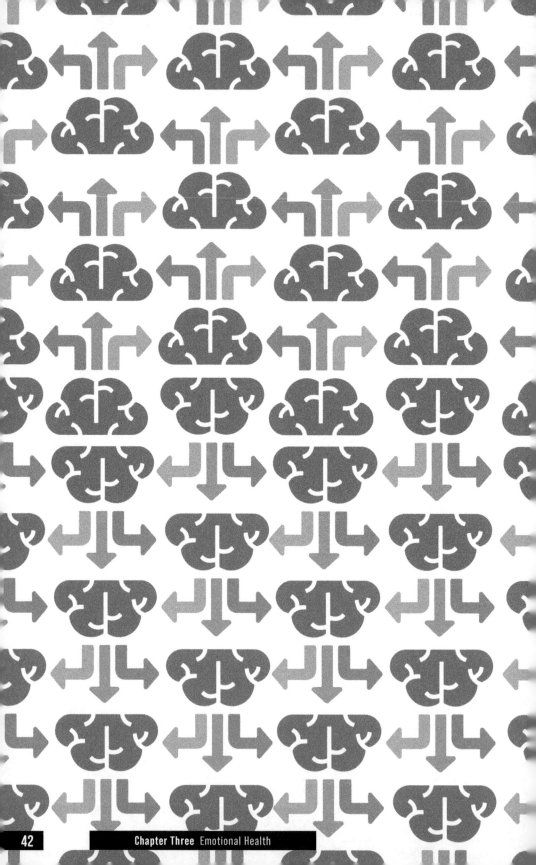

THE ABILITY TO MAKE GOOD DECISIONS

Good decision making can be a challenge for people of any age. How do you decide what's a good idea and what's a bad one? How do you know who's a good friend and who can hurt you? Experience teaches you.

Deciding to skip school to help someone in a desperate situation may be a good idea as a one-time event. The positive or negative consequence will be the proof of the wisdom of each one of your choices. Deciding to skip school or even a class to smoke or drink, however, can end up with outcomes you didn't intend or want. And these consequences may have a lasting impact. You may get punished. You may get away with it.

What kinds of impact on your next decision will getting punished or getting away with it have? On the other hand, deciding to work extra hard for a test, deciding to help a friend, or do chores for the family can have many benefits with an impact just as lasting. Healthy decision making is shaped by what happens after you have acted on your decisions.

WHERE DOES DECISION MAKING COME FROM

Decision Making comes from the part of your brain that governs judgment. From age 13 to 25, the young brain is intensively shaped and reshaped based on its experiences. Connections within the brain that are used the most become stronger, while those that are not used much get weaker. That's the reason getting involved in challenging intellectual, athletic, and social activities will prepare your brain for your adult life.

The last region of the brain to develop is the Pre-Frontal Cortex which governs judgment. We'll learn more about the brain in Chapter 5. Teens have a lot of energy and emotion, but without the ability to predict outcomes and plan accordingly, they may make choices such as using drugs and alcohol that will hurt them for their entire life.

THE ABILITY TO MANAGE EMOTIONS

Your physical and social lives affect your emotional life. No matter how old or young you are, your moods are affected by the people around you, events that are occurring, how well you may be performing ... and even the weather.

HORMONES ARE EMOTIONAL INFLUENCERS

Hormones that haven't been active until puberty affect teens' moods, emotions, and impulses as well as their body. Teens experience mood swings that are caused by fluctuations in Estrogen, Progesterone, and Testosterone. These are the Sex Hormones, and they can make you feel as if you have been taken over by aliens. Many teens feel that the changes in their body, moods and thoughts are unwanted, freakish, and even unnatural. When teens are unsure about their gender identity, hormones can complicate their emotions.

4 QUESTIONS TO ASK YOURSELF ABOUT YOUR MOODS

1. How many times a day do you feel different emotions?

2. Is your life a roller coaster of conflicting emotions?

3. Does your whole personality seem to change overnight?

4. Do you feel depressed and anxious about every little thing?

EMOTION WHEEL

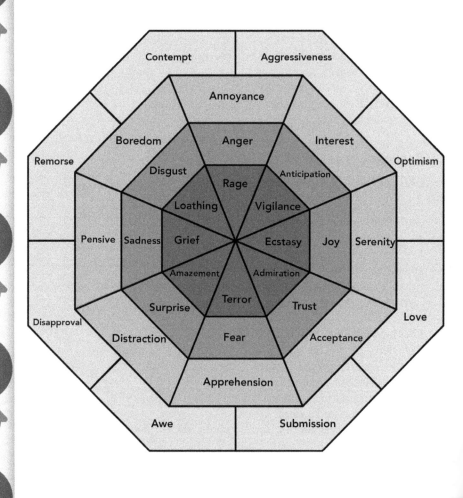

HOW MANY EMOTIONS
ARE THERE

Researchers have identified 27 Emotions, most of which are interconnected. Emotions can lift you up or cast you down in just a second. We may not be able to identify all our emotions as we experience them, but they influence how we act and what we do whether we can identify our feelings or not. Happy, sad, scared, worried, excited, unhappy, mad, emotions play a big part in our daily life. No one escapes feelings. The eight basic feelings are shown here. You can see by the graph that each one of the eight basic feelings has different gradations with different descriptions of emotions we will be feeling throughout the day. Emotions are powerful. They can lead to love or hate, kindness or violence. Our experiences with people shape our feelings, but other factors also influence our moods and emotional health. Substances, alcohol, and the medicines we take alter our feelings and moods. Nutrition, exercise and hormones also affect mood and the way we feel about things. Everyone needs to learn how to manage emotions so they don't become overwhelming, take over, and keep us stuck.

" FIVE THINGS YOU SHOULD KNOW ABOUT STRESS

1.Stress affects everyone Everyone experiences stress from time to time. There are different types of stress—all of which carry physical and mental health risks. A stressor may be a one-time or short-term occurrence, or it can happen repeatedly over a long time. Some people may cope with stress more effectively and recover from stressful events more quickly than others.Examples of stress include:

- Routine stress related to the pressures of school, work, family, and other daily responsibilities.

- Stress brought about by a sudden negative change, such as losing a job, divorce, or illness.

- Traumatic stress experienced during an event such as a major accident, war, assault, or natural disaster where people may be in danger of being seriously hurt or killed. People who experience traumatic stress may have very distressing temporary emotional and physical symptoms, but most recover naturally soon after.

2.Not all stress is bad In a dangerous situation, stress signals the body to prepare to face a threat or flee to safety. In these situations, your pulse quickens, you breathe faster, your muscles tense, and your brain uses more oxygen and increases activity—all functions aimed at survival and in response to stress. In non-life-threatening situations, stress can motivate people, such as when they need to take a test or interview for a new job.

3.Long-term stress can harm your health Coping with the impact of chronic stress can be challenging. Because the source of long-term stress is more constant than acute stress, the body never receives a clear signal to return to normal functioning.

With chronic stress, those same lifesaving reactions in the body can disturb the immune, digestive, cardiovascular, sleep, and reproductive systems. Some people may experience mainly digestive symptoms, while others may have headaches, sleeplessness, sadness, anger, or irritability.

Over time, continued strain on your body from stress may contribute to serious health problems, such as heart disease, high blood pressure, diabetes, and other illnesses, including mental disorders such as depression or anxiety.

4.There are ways to manage stress If you take practical steps to manage your stress, you may reduce the risk of negative health effects. Here are some tips that may help you to cope with stress:

- Be observant. Recognize the signs of your body's response to stress, such as difficulty sleeping, increased alcohol and other substance use, being easily angered, feeling depressed, and having low energy.

- Get regular exercise. Just 30 minutes per day of walking can help boost your mood and improve your health.

- Try a relaxing activity. Explore relaxation or wellness programs, which may incorporate meditation, muscle relaxation, or breathing exercises. Schedule regular times for these and other healthy and relaxing activities.

- Set goals and priorities. Decide what must get done now and what can wait. Learn to say "no" to new tasks if you start to feel like you're taking on too much. Try to be mindful of what you have accomplished at the end of the day, not what you have been unable to do.

- Stay connected. You are not alone. Keep in touch with people who can provide emotional support and practical help. To reduce stress, ask for help from friends, family, and community or religious organizations.

5.If you're overwhelmed by stress, ask for help from a health professional. You should seek help right away if you have suicidal thoughts, are overwhelmed, feel you cannot cope, or are using drugs or alcohol more frequently as a result of stress. Your doctor may be able to provide a recommendation. Resources are available to help you find a mental health provider.

SOURCE : **National Institute on Drug Abuse; National Institutes of Health; U.S. Department of Health and Human Services.**

THE ABILITY TO MANAGE STRESS

What is Stress anyway? We hear about stress all the time, and we sure feel it in so many areas of our lives. In fact, stress is one of our constant, unwelcome companions throughout our whole life. Relationships that include getting along with all kinds people, doing our work on time, eating the right kinds of food, even getting enough sleep can all cause stress. In short, stress is pressures, worry, and anxiety. We all feel stress from so many sources.

Each of us needs an office manager of stress. Can we study enough for the test? Can we please our coach, can we do well and succeed? Do we have enough money? Can we even be ready for school on time? Can we perform our work well and make friends? How about getting enough exercise if we're not in a sports program? How about the worry we have about family members and their financial problems? Everyone has areas of worry and concern. What do you worry about the most?

Is worrying a good thing when we don't have control of everything in our lives?

Worry affects our mood, our self-esteem, our performance, even our physical health, so it can get in the way of our relationships and work. Here are 12 tips for managing stress. You can see that physical and emotional health are connected.

1. Eat Healthy Foods When you think about getting a balanced diet and what you're eating, you're less stressed about other things.

2. Get Enough Rest Being alert and well rested helps you to organize and stay on top of things.

3. Exercise Regularly Your body fights stress best when it is fit.

4. Avoid Marijuana, Illegal Drugs, Tobacco products, Alcohol, Gaming, and Social Media as a way of reducing stress. Addictive substances and behaviors derail you and alter brain function, sometimes in lasting ways.

5. Have A Sense Of Humor and laugh to reduce stress and feel happier.

6. Learn To Say No Often requests from friends and family members only add more pressure to your life. Saying no teaches you how to have boundaries.

7. Have A Few Go-To Friends Teachers, And Family Members you can talk to who can help you with problems and concerns.

8. Communicate Appropriately with others by being assertive, not by getting angry and defensive or being passive. Both fighting and holding back feelings are stressful. Learning to communicate effectively clarifies relationships and lowers stress.

9. Accept that there are things you can't control If you know you can't fix it, worrying about it only adds to your stress.

10. Learn To Manage Your Time Effectively Wasted time produces stress when tasks haven't been accomplished.

11. Spend Regular Time On Your Hobby which can be art, music, science, sports, nature. Hobbies are great stress-reducers and promote self-expression.

12. Take A Time Out To Relax If you don't know how to relax, think meditation, soft music, yoga, pets, or just a short nap to give your busy brain a rest.

THE ABILITY TO SOLVE PROBLEMS

Solutions is another name for Problem solving, and it is the basis of all human development and civilization. Humans had to figure out how to hunt and gather food, how to develop tools, how to build structures and travel long distances. There have been amazing inventions of every kind that came from the need to solve a problem. On a personal level, too, we're always looking for solutions: to get things done, to get somewhere, to fix things that have gone wrong. Solutions is a word that shows all the ways our brains have to work to figure out and implement what's going on, and what needs to be done about it. We problem solve all day every day. When we problem solve, we use the part of our brain that develops critical thinking.

WHERE DOES PROBLEM SOLVING COME FROM

Problem Solving comes from the Frontal Lobe of your brain, which is like the chip in the computer that is you. There are six sections inside the brain: Frontal Lobe, Parietal Lobe, Occipital Lobe, Temporal Lobe, Cerebellum, and the Brain Stem. Problem Solving is an important function governed by the frontal lobe. The frontal lobe links and integrates all components of behavior at the highest level. Emotion and social adjustment, impulse control, abstract reasoning, sustained attention, and insight are all located here. This part of the brain can easily be injured or damaged.

6 TIPS FOR PROBLEM SOLVING

1. Identify the information you have and what information is missing

2. Ask questions to fill in the gaps

3. Identify possible solutions, think about the problem in different ways

4. Write it out

5. Evaluate potential solutions

6. Practice going through the process to build your confidence and competence

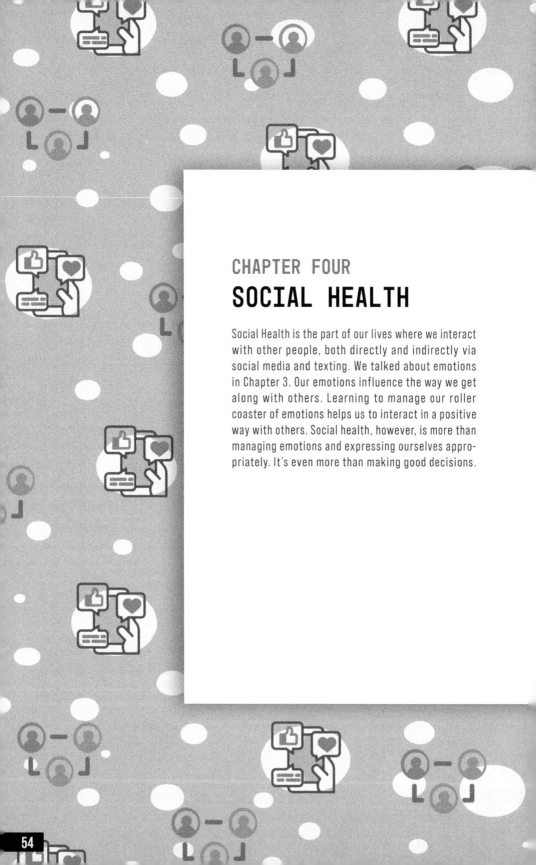

CHAPTER FOUR

SOCIAL HEALTH

Social Health is the part of our lives where we interact with other people, both directly and indirectly via social media and texting. We talked about emotions in Chapter 3. Our emotions influence the way we get along with others. Learning to manage our roller coaster of emotions helps us to interact in a positive way with others. Social health, however, is more than managing emotions and expressing ourselves appropriately. It's even more than making good decisions.

Do you know the ways you influence Other people

You have both positive and negative impact on other people

What you say and how you act matters to them

You have social choices just like choosing your style of dress or what you eat

There are consequences to your social choices

HOW DO YOU MAKE
OTHERS FEEL?

ARE YOU JUDGMENTAL
OR COMPASSIONATE ?

WHAT IS YOUR
PERSONAL STYLE?

Social Health means learning how to use emotional health tools to cope with your relationships. Every day we have dozens of interactions with people. Being socially healthy means we understand that our demeanor and actions influence how well we get along with others. When our interactions are negative, we can adjust our behavior for better results.

HOW MANY RELATIONSHIPS DO YOU HAVE

Just take a minute to think of all the people you have to deal with every day. Teachers, parents, schoolmates, friends, family members, coaches, and all those around you on buses, in stores, on sports teams, at jobs. Not everyone is a friend, or safe to be with. Being socially healthy sometimes means managing difficult relationships not just with family and friends, but with all kinds of people: People we like and want to like us, and those we don't like, or fear, and want to avoid.

EMOTIONAL HEALTH IN SOCIAL HEALTH

Being Socially Healthy means we can evaluate all our relationships and manage them carefully. We want to make and keep a few good friends and have loving family relationships. But we also have to keep ourselves and others around us safe from abuse or harm.

The emotional components in Chapter 3 work with social components in Chapter 4 to help us figure out what's going on with all our relationships so we can make healthy decisions. We also have to manage the relationships we have digitally. Sometimes we may feel we don't fit in at school, or even in our own families. You may wonder where, or with whom, you belong. Social health components determine what kind of person you are and want to be.

HELPING OTHERS

It feels good to be useful. Lending a hand also makes people feel good about you. In every situation, you have the choice to help, to do nothing, or to make things worse. You can disrupt a class or help the teacher by being quiet. You can help your mother or father or siblings with errands or chores, or you can wait for others to do the work. You can help in many different ways. Have you seen the video of the man who jumps into a frozen lake to save a drowning dog? Or the teen who climbs a tree to rescue a kitten in a storm, or the girls who collect and give food to the hungry? These are dramatic examples of rescue, but even the smallest kinds of assistance can be seen as rescues that enhance someone's life, or your whole community.

HOW HELPFUL ARE YOU

Do you feel like helping the teacher when chairs or furniture need moving? Do you help with the laundry or meals at home? Do you help a friend with homework or sports? Do you help a disabled person cross the street? How useful you are to others is an indicator of one kind of social health because being helpful to others brings positive results in their caring for you.

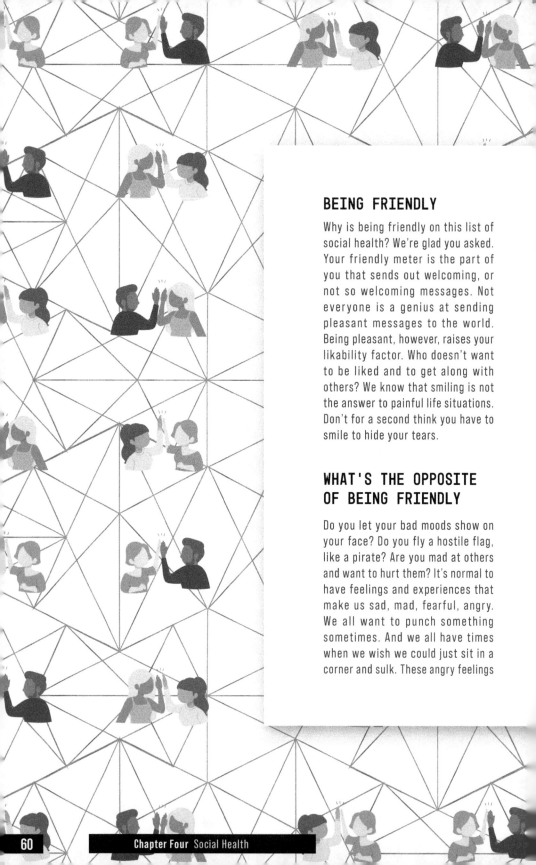

BEING FRIENDLY

Why is being friendly on this list of social health? We're glad you asked. Your friendly meter is the part of you that sends out welcoming, or not so welcoming messages. Not everyone is a genius at sending pleasant messages to the world. Being pleasant, however, raises your likability factor. Who doesn't want to be liked and to get along with others? We know that smiling is not the answer to painful life situations. Don't for a second think you have to smile to hide your tears.

WHAT'S THE OPPOSITE OF BEING FRIENDLY

Do you let your bad moods show on your face? Do you fly a hostile flag, like a pirate? Are you mad at others and want to hurt them? It's normal to have feelings and experiences that make us sad, mad, fearful, angry. We all want to punch something sometimes. And we all have times when we wish we could just sit in a corner and sulk. These angry feelings

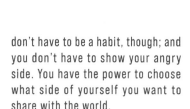

don't have to be a habit, though; and you don't have to show your angry side. You have the power to choose what side of yourself you want to share with the world.

BEING FRIENDLY DOESN'T MEAN YOU'RE A PUSHOVER

Being friendly doesn't mean you make friends with everyone or let others push you around. Being friendly means you're pleasant and open. You don't measure the people you meet by their appearance, their size, the color of their skin or where they're from. A healthy reaction to students who are different from you is welcoming, not fearful or hostile. Healthy people are pleasant to their extended family and the people with whom they interact every day. Being pleasant is a habit that anyone can develop. It's what will make you likable. Being friendly means smiling, not scowling. Being friendly helps improve the mood of everyone around you and opens the door for friendship.

FRIENDLY DOES NOT MEAN FRIENDSHIP

Being friendly doesn't mean you should make friends with everyone. No one can, or should, open up or offer friendship or share feelings with people who could harm you either emotionally or physically. Here's where problem solving, which uses the critical thinking part of your brain, and decision making as described in Chapter 3 work together to help you set your boundaries with other people.

CONCERN FOR OTHERS

This Social Health component is where Empathy comes in. Empathy means identifying with other people's feelings and showing compassion. Empathy is more than being friendly and pleasant. Concern for others adds kindness to the social picture. Kindness is different from being nice. We can act nice to get along with others, but concern means we can relate to other people and their feelings. For good social health, we need to have or develop the concern and caring component for others.

WHAT IS THE OPPOSITE OF CONCERN FOR OTHERS

Teasing, Bullying, Calling People Names are the opposite of caring about them. We see lack of empathy everywhere: In the world, in our country, in our politics, at school, even at home sometimes. When people don't look like you or act like you and you dislike them for their differences, that is the opposite of compassion.

Ignoring People In Trouble is the opposite of concern. Intolerance is also the opposite of caring. How do we distinguish between identification, which is healthy, and lack of tolerance and compassion, which is not healthy?

WHAT DOES CONCERN LOOK LIKE

Feeling the pain of someone who's lonely or hurt is the first step to concern. You may care about animals or the environment. You may have a deep identification with your culture, your politics, your religion, and your country. You may care about your family and their needs. That is compassion related to personal identification. Having compassion for those who aren't in that group is an important component of empathy. You don't have to like people to have concern for what's happening to them.

FAMILY & OTHER RELATIONSHIPS

Making friends, getting along with our families, teachers, co-workers are another important component of social health. Relationships matter because they affect all the other areas of our lives. If you don't have a good relationship with your parents, it's hard to have good relationships with your teachers. You may form friendships with people who hurt you. Or you may not be able to make friends at all. Relationships are challenging at every age. Not everyone is easy to get along with. Learning how to make and have friends takes effort and experience.

In the best of all possible worlds, we would have loving families, caring friends, friendly teachers and a good boss at work. We'd know how to fit in and be popular. But almost no one lives in the best of all worlds.

6 REASONS YOU MIGHT NEED HELP

1. Not everyone has parents who teach them healthy social skills.

2. Not everyone lives in one place; military families, for example, move often.

3. Divorce, homelessness, and food instability all contribute to difficulty making friends.

4. Substance use by a sibling or parent can make trusting others a problem.

5. Feeling that you don't fit in, don't look or act like people around you can be isolating.

6. Anxiety and lack of confidence can also hold you back.

HEALTHY RELATIONSHIPS DEVELOP WITH EXPERIENCE

We all have different skills, different interests, different personalities. We're different from each other. And we get along with others well or badly on a sliding scale. For example, you may get along at home, but have difficulty knowing what to say or how to act at school. Rest assured that whatever problems you have, you are not alone. Know that you can bond with other people through common interests, common talents, cultural affiliations, your religion, and your studies.

" WHAT'S A HEALTHY RELATIONSHIP

Strong, healthy relationships are important for a happy life. Your connections with family members, friends, boyfriends/girlfriends, and others affect your mental, emotional, and even physical health.

Take relationships in the teen years, for example. Healthy relationships with parents and friends can help a teen become increasingly independent and develop a sense of personal identity and strong self-esteem.

So, how can you tell if a relationship is positive for you?

Here are some signs of a healthy relationship:

- You feel good about yourself around the other person. You feel safe talking about how you feel. You listen to each other. You feel valued, and each of you trusts the other person.

-Conflicts, which are normal, don't turn into personal attacks. You can disagree without hurting each other and make decisions together.

- The other person motivates you to do positive things like succeed in school and be involved in extracurricular activities.

- The other person doesn't encourage you to do risky or self-destructive things like drive recklessly or use drugs. In fact, having healthy relationships can reduce the odds that a person will use drugs.

- You feel physically safe around that person.

At any age, your relationships matter, and having healthy relationships with others starts with liking yourself. Treat yourself the way a good friend would treat you. Know that you deserve to be treated well by others.

If you or a friend needs help with an unhealthy relationship, contact the **National Domestic Violence Hotline** at *www.thehotline.org* or call *1-800-799-SAFE.*

SOURCE: National Institute on Drug Abuse; National Institutes of Health; U.S. Department of Health and Human Services.

"

SOCIAL MEDIA

Texting, Gaming, and Social Media are temptations that affect everyone. Social media's benefit is that it connects you with others and informs you about what's going on. It's normal to feel some confusion about your many different kinds of face-to-face relationships, but digital relationships may not be real or healthy. Social media can be used as a form of expression and endless entertainment, but it has its dark side, too.

8 WAYS SOCIAL MEDIA CAN HURT YOU

1. Social media feeds are confusing—there's no way know what's true and what isn't.

2. You can get plenty of the wrong information.

3. You can be led in the wrong direction by people who can harm you.

4. You can be hurt by the things people say.

5. You can feel less than or left out.

6. You can fall into a meme-induced trance that lasts for hours and wastes time.

7. You can get addicted to so many kinds of information.

8. Too much social media, texting, and gaming can actually cause depression and even more anxiety, especially at night.

4 QUESTIONS TO ASK YOURSELF

1. How many hours do you spend each day scrolling through your feed?

2. How often do you compare yourself to the people you follow?

3. How often do you feel depressed after seeing other people's exciting adventures?

4. How often do you feel insecure and left out?

If you don't know how much time you spend online, try using the timer on the phone or device you're using. There is a screen time feature on some phones that shows how much time you have spent on each application. You'll be surprised how much time goes by.

4 TIPS TO SNAP OUT OF IT

1. If you feel negative thoughts creeping into your head while scrolling through someone's perfect posts, close the app and get active.

2. Catch up on homework or do something creative.

3. Talk to someone in person.

4. Try turning off your phone, tablet, and gaming devices, a couple hours before bed. A good night's sleep is essential for mental health.

" COPING WITH TRAUMATIC EVENTS

A traumatic event is a shocking, scary, or dangerous experience that can affect someone emotionally and physically. Experiences like natural disasters (such as hurricanes, earthquakes, and floods), acts of violence (such as assault, abuse, terrorist attacks, and mass shootings), as well as car crashes and other accidents can all be traumatic. Researchers are investigating the factors that help people cope or that increase their risk for other physical or mental health problems following a traumatic event.

WARNING SIGNS

Responses to trauma can be immediate or delayed, brief or prolonged. Most people have intense responses immediately following, and often for several weeks or months after a traumatic event. These responses can include:

- Feeling anxious, sad, or angry

- Trouble concentrating and sleeping

- Continually thinking about what happened

For most people, these are normal and expected responses and generally lessen with time.

In some cases, these responses continue for a longer period of time and interfere with everyday life. If they are interfering with daily life or are not getting better over time, it is important to seek professional help. Some signs that an individual may need help include:

- Worrying a lot or feeling very anxious, sad, or fearful

- Crying often

- Having trouble thinking clearly

- Having frightening thoughts or flashbacks, reliving the experience

- Feeling angry, resentful, or irritable

- Having nightmares or difficulty sleeping

- Avoiding places or people that bring back disturbing memories and responses.

- Becoming isolated from family & friends

Teens may also develop disruptive, disrespectful, or destructive behaviors. Older children and teens may feel guilty for not preventing injury or deaths. They may also have thoughts of revenge.

Physical responses to trauma may also mean that an individual needs help. Physical symptoms may include:

- Headaches

- Stomach pain and digestive issues

- Feeling tired

- Racing heart and sweating

- Being very jumpy and easily startled

Individuals who have a mental health condition or who have had traumatic experiences in the past, who face ongoing stress, or who lack support from friends and family may be more likely to develop more severe symptoms and need additional help. Some people turn to alcohol or other drugs to cope with their symptoms. Although substance use may seem to relieve symptoms temporarily, it can also lead to new problems and get in the way of recovery.

WAYS TO COPE

Healthy ways of coping include:

- Avoiding alcohol and other drugs;

- Spending time with loved ones and trusted friends who are supportive; and

- Trying to maintain normal routines for meals, exercise, and sleep.

- In general, staying active is a good way to cope with stressful feelings.

SOURCE: National Institute on Drug Abuse; National Institutes of Health; U.S. Department of Health and Human Services.

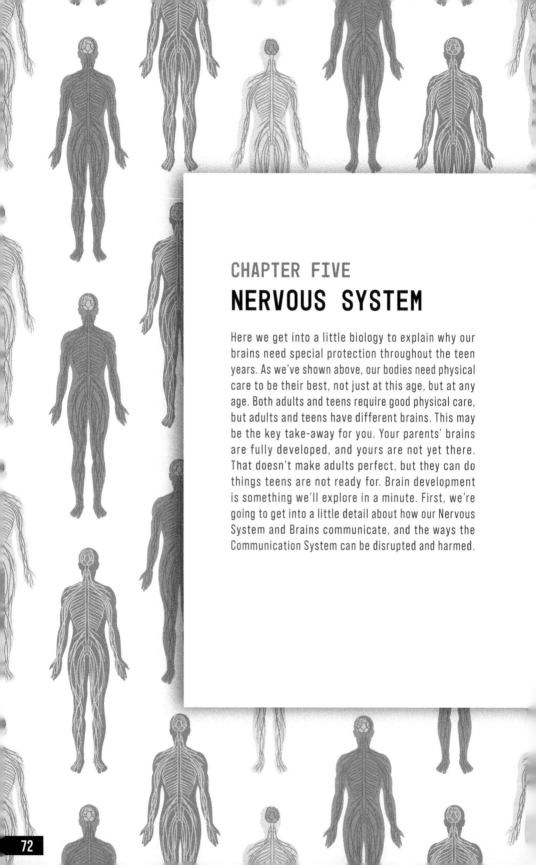

CHAPTER FIVE
NERVOUS SYSTEM

Here we get into a little biology to explain why our brains need special protection throughout the teen years. As we've shown above, our bodies need physical care to be their best, not just at this age, but at any age. Both adults and teens require good physical care, but adults and teens have different brains. This may be the key take-away for you. Your parents' brains are fully developed, and yours are not yet there. That doesn't make adults perfect, but they can do things teens are not ready for. Brain development is something we'll explore in a minute. First, we're going to get into a little detail about how our Nervous System and Brains communicate, and the ways the Communication System can be disrupted and harmed.

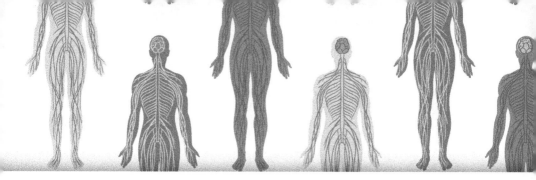

All the organs in the human body comprise a complicated transportation system that keeps us running smoothly. The Nervous System is the master control that tells all our organs what to do. At its most basic level, the nervous system is the communication system between the entire body and the brain. It is the system which carries signals from the brain to the rest of the body, and back.

HOW DOES THE NERVOUS SYSTEM WORK?

WHY ARE ADULT AND TEEN BRAINS NOT THE SAME?

WHAT HAPPENS WHEN THE NERVOUS SYSTEM IS DISRUPTED?

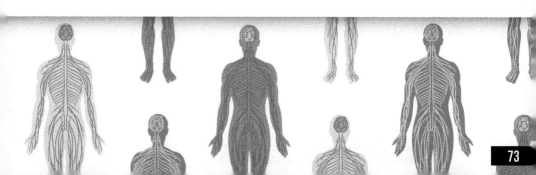

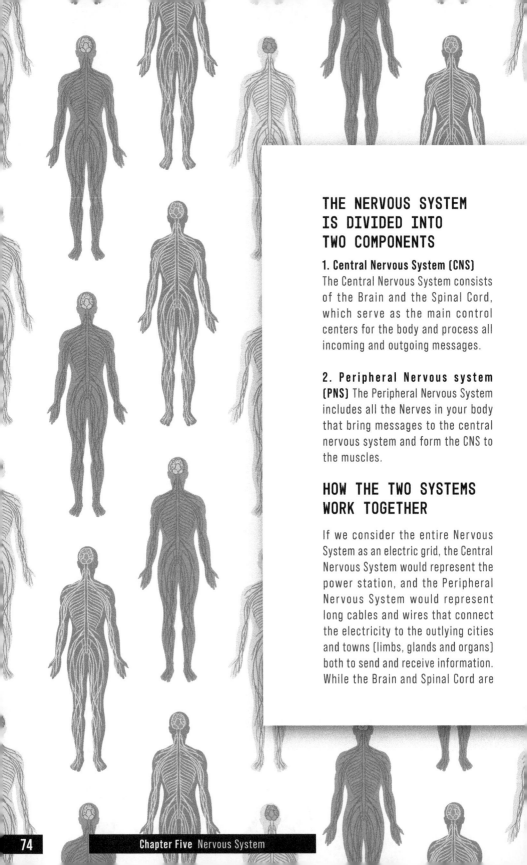

THE NERVOUS SYSTEM IS DIVIDED INTO TWO COMPONENTS

1. Central Nervous System (CNS)
The Central Nervous System consists of the Brain and the Spinal Cord, which serve as the main control centers for the body and process all incoming and outgoing messages.

2. Peripheral Nervous system (PNS)
The Peripheral Nervous System includes all the Nerves in your body that bring messages to the central nervous system and form the CNS to the muscles.

HOW THE TWO SYSTEMS WORK TOGETHER

If we consider the entire Nervous System as an electric grid, the Central Nervous System would represent the power station, and the Peripheral Nervous System would represent long cables and wires that connect the electricity to the outlying cities and towns (limbs, glands and organs) both to send and receive information. While the Brain and Spinal Cord are

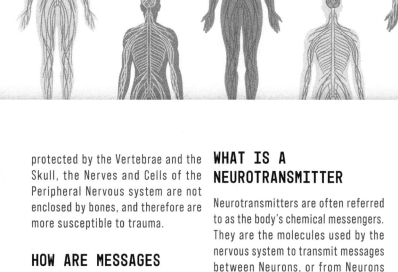

protected by the Vertebrae and the Skull, the Nerves and Cells of the Peripheral Nervous system are not enclosed by bones, and therefore are more susceptible to trauma.

HOW ARE MESSAGES COMMUNICATED IN THE BRAIN

The organs in the Nervous System are made up of cells called Neurons. Neurons are responsible for carrying information throughout the human body. Using electrical and chemical signals, neurons help coordinate all of the necessary functions of life. Each neuron is connected to another 1,000 neurons, creating an incredibly complex network of communication. Neurons are considered the basic units of the nervous system. It has been estimated that there are around 86 billion neurons in the brain. To reach this vast number a developing fetus must create 250,000 neurons per minute. In stages of growth in Chapter 6, we will see that a pruning of neurons will take place in the teen brain, when connections that are not used as much get weaker.

WHAT IS A NEUROTRANSMITTER

Neurotransmitters are often referred to as the body's chemical messengers. They are the molecules used by the nervous system to transmit messages between Neurons, or from Neurons to Muscles.

HOW DO NEURONS COMMUNICATE WITH EACH OTHER

Communication between two Neurons happens in the Synaptic Cleft [the small gap between the Synapses of neurons. Here, electrical signals that have traveled along the Axon are briefly converted into chemical ones through the release of Neurotransmitters, causing a specific response in the receiving neuron.

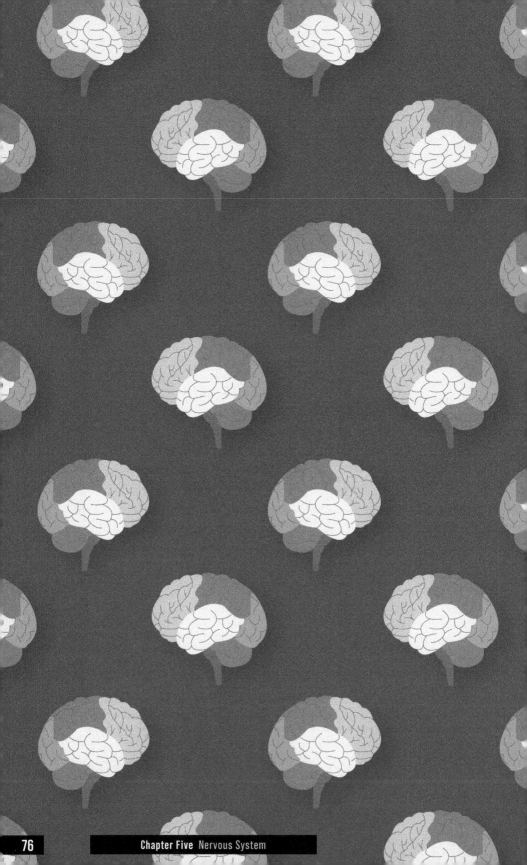

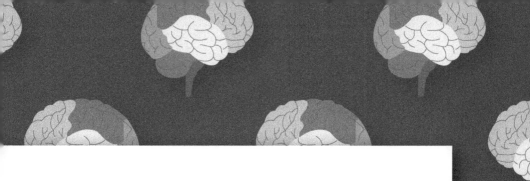

THE BRAIN

Your Brain is like a computer that controls every part of your physical body and thinking. It evaluates information through touch, sight, hearing, taste, and smell and is also responsible for your intelligence, creativity, emotions, and memory. Your brain is complex and is protected by the hard shell of your skull.

YOUR BRAIN HAS 3 MAJOR COMPONENTS

1. Cerebrum The largest lobe is composed of the right and left sides of your brain. It interprets touch, vision, hearing, speech, reasoning, emotions, learning, and can control your movements.

2. Cerebellum The second largest lobe coordinates muscle movement, posture, and balance.

3. Brain Stem The bridge that connects your brain to your spinal cord. The brain stem transfers your brain's signals to the rest of your body. It also keeps you breathing, controls your heart rate, sleeping cycles, and body temperature.

FUN FACT ABOUT THE LEFT AND RIGHT SIDES OF YOUR BRAIN

The Left Side of the Brain controls the right side of your body and hosts the skills of speech, arithmetic, and writing. The Right Side of the brain controls the left side of the body and is responsible for creativity, spatial relations, and art and music skills. Are you a right or left-brain kind of person?

THE BRAIN

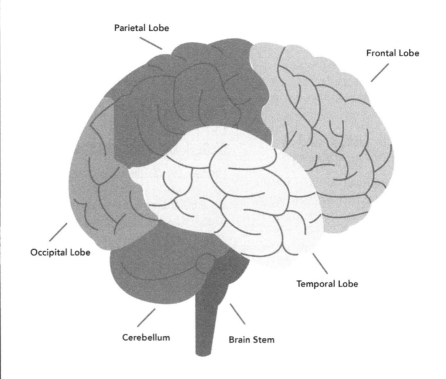

Parietal Lobe

Frontal Lobe

Occipital Lobe

Temporal Lobe

Cerebellum

Brain Stem

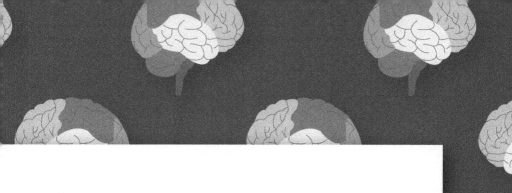

EACH HEMISPHERE OF YOUR BRAIN HAS 4 LOBES

1.Frontal Lobe helps to shape your personality, behavior, emotions, judgment, planning, problem-solving, speech and writing, body movement, intelligence, concentration, and self-awareness.

2. Parietal Lobe interprets language and words, your sense of touch (which includes pain and temperature), signals from vision, hearing, motor, and memory; and spatial and visual perception.

3. Occipital Lobe translates vision, which includes color, light, and movement.

4. Temporal Lobe computes language, memory, hearing, and helps you organize your thoughts and memories.

Like a computer, our brain stores our memories and the important data that we take in each day. There are three phases to remembering something that had once happened: encoding (figuring out what's important), storing, and recalling.

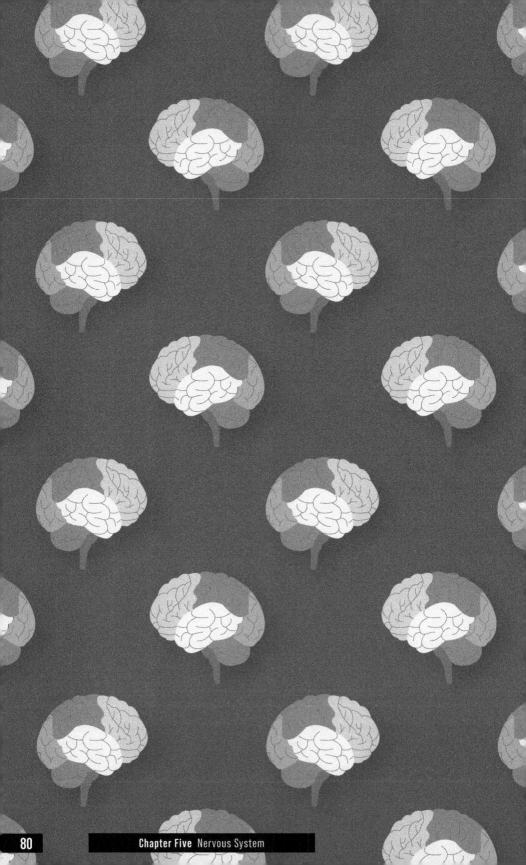

THERE ARE 3 KINDS OF MEMORY

1. Short Term Memory is generally in the Prefrontal Cortex. This is where you can store up to one minute of a memory and up to 7 items. Think about when you first learned your locker combination. That probably wasn't memorized the first, or even fourth, time you tried opening the locked door.

2. Long Term Memories are in the Hippocampus of your Temporal Lobe. It works when you want to remember something for a longer period of time, like a speech you may have to make for a class or a monologue for drama club. This area has unlimited storage and can hold your own memories, facts, and data.

3. Skill Memory is processed in the Cerebellum. It stores memories like tying your shoes or buckling your belt or riding a bike. Has anyone ever said to you, "It's like riding a bike," meaning information you won't ever forget.

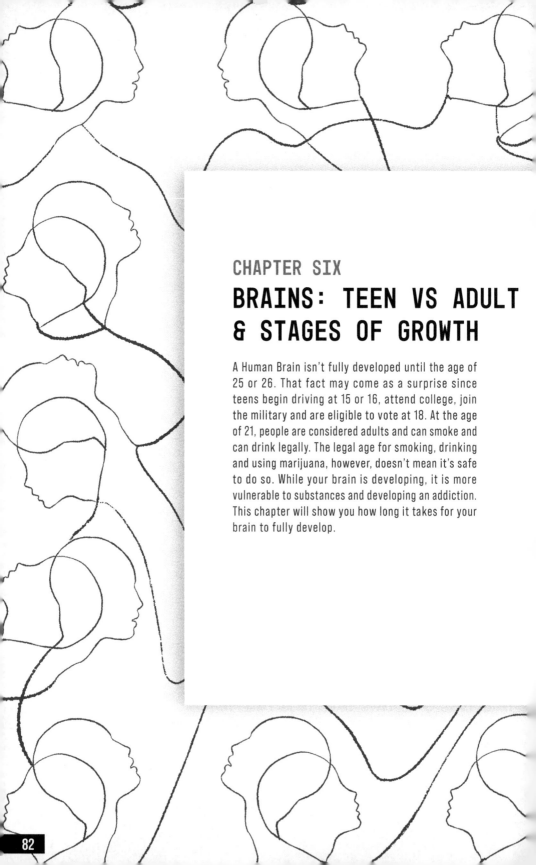

CHAPTER SIX

BRAINS: TEEN VS ADULT & STAGES OF GROWTH

A Human Brain isn't fully developed until the age of 25 or 26. That fact may come as a surprise since teens begin driving at 15 or 16, attend college, join the military and are eligible to vote at 18. At the age of 21, people are considered adults and can smoke and can drink legally. The legal age for smoking, drinking and using marijuana, however, doesn't mean it's safe to do so. While your brain is developing, it is more vulnerable to substances and developing an addiction. This chapter will show you how long it takes for your brain to fully develop.

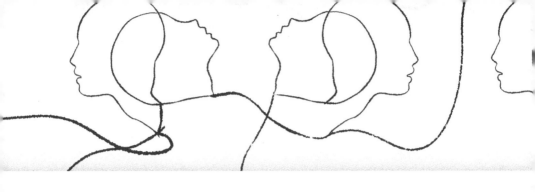

WHY DOES BRAIN
DEVELOPMENT TAKE
SO LONG?

WHEN WILL YOUR BRAIN
BE FULLY DEVELOPED?

WHY IS THE TEEN BRAIN
VULNERABLE TO
SUBSTANCE ADDICTION?

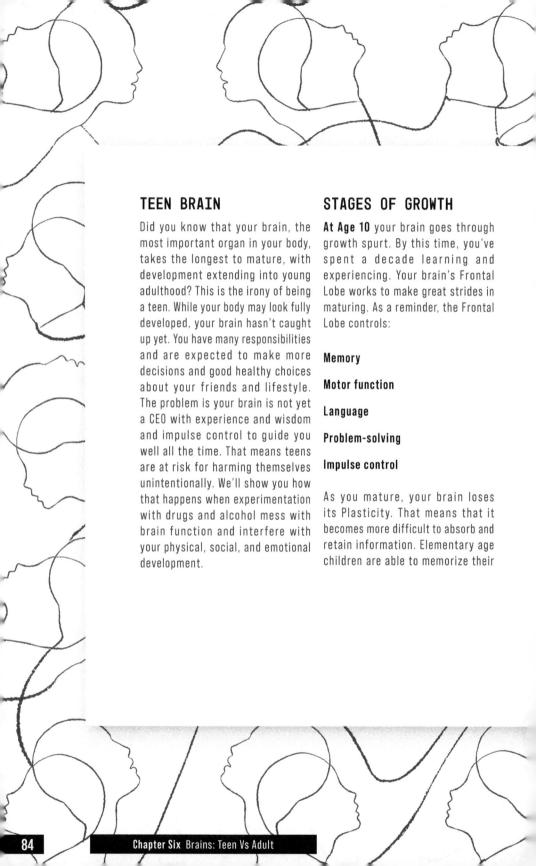

TEEN BRAIN

Did you know that your brain, the most important organ in your body, takes the longest to mature, with development extending into young adulthood? This is the irony of being a teen. While your body may look fully developed, your brain hasn't caught up yet. You have many responsibilities and are expected to make more decisions and good healthy choices about your friends and lifestyle. The problem is your brain is not yet a CEO with experience and wisdom and impulse control to guide you well all the time. That means teens are at risk for harming themselves unintentionally. We'll show you how that happens when experimentation with drugs and alcohol mess with brain function and interfere with your physical, social, and emotional development.

STAGES OF GROWTH

At Age 10 your brain goes through growth spurt. By this time, you've spent a decade learning and experiencing. Your brain's Frontal Lobe works to make great strides in maturing. As a reminder, the Frontal Lobe controls:

Memory

Motor function

Language

Problem-solving

Impulse control

As you mature, your brain loses its Plasticity. That means that it becomes more difficult to absorb and retain information. Elementary age children are able to memorize their

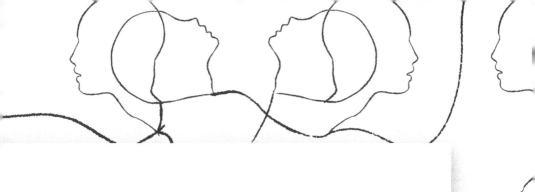

studies more easily because their brain is still forming, and the memory portions are maturing. Along with the Frontal Lobe, the Hippocampus, which is in the lower region of the brain, also strengthens. This way, memories are more easily transferred between the long and short-term memory locations.

Ages 13 TO 15 the size and function of your Brain increase, particularly in the Frontal Cortex where your motor and special perception areas are found. This is also when the Pituitary Gland starts releasing hormones into your bloodstream to trigger other organs to release their own Hormones. These hormones kick start your Reproductive capability and sexual growth. We've talked about the impact of hormones on your emotional life. It may feel like the world and your emotional life is out of control.

Age 17 your Brain goes through another growth spurt. Again, the Frontal Lobes grow, which increases the Synaptic Connections. At this point, your brain is close to, if not already, the size of an average adult brain: 3 pounds, but not yet finished maturing.

Age 18 your brain undergoes processes called "pruning." This is when it begins to shed the weaker connections between Neurons. Remember how many neurons had to be created by fetuses in the womb? As the brain develops, more changes are occurring. Around this time, your Synapses drop from 1,000 trillion to 500 trillion—the amount an eight-month-old baby has. See how complicated brain development is?

One of the last parts of your brain to develop is your Prefrontal Cortex. The Prefrontal Cortex is responsible for decision-making and the ability to think ahead. Thinking, or planning ahead, means having the ability to distinguish between Risk and Reward Choices. This is where teens are most at risk for making unhealthy decisions.

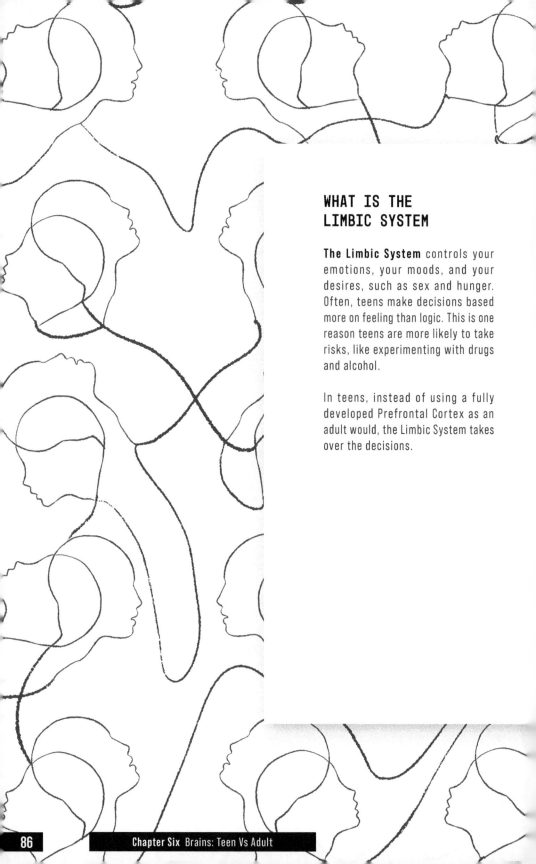

WHAT IS THE LIMBIC SYSTEM

The Limbic System controls your emotions, your moods, and your desires, such as sex and hunger. Often, teens make decisions based more on feeling than logic. This is one reason teens are more likely to take risks, like experimenting with drugs and alcohol.

In teens, instead of using a fully developed Prefrontal Cortex as an adult would, the Limbic System takes over the decisions.

THE LIMBIC SYSTEM

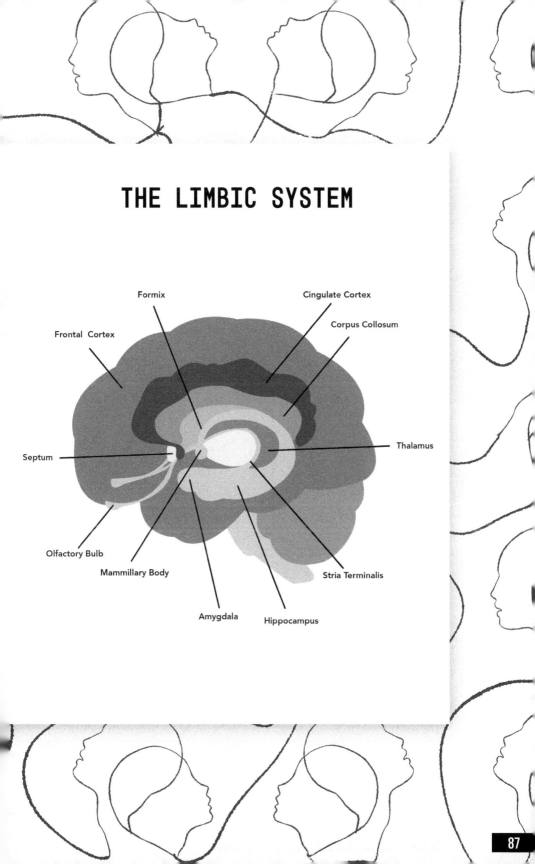

Formix

Cingulate Cortex

Corpus Collosum

Frontal Cortex

Septum

Thalamus

Olfactory Bulb

Mammillary Body

Stria Terminalis

Amygdala

Hippocampus

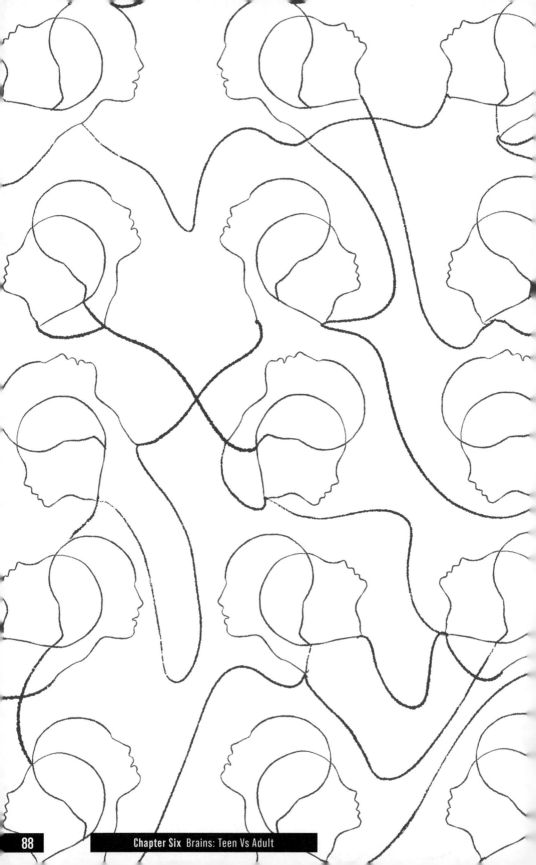

DRUGS & ALCOHOL HAVE A GREATER IMPACT ON THE TEEN BRAIN

When your Brain is still developing, it is extremely vulnerable to the effects of substances. Neurons need a healthy atmosphere to grow and generate Synapses which help exchange information quickly and enhance your ability to make healthy and safe choices into the adult years.

ADULT BRAIN

Neurons cover (or, Myelinate) an adult's brain. The neurons are protected and are able to transport messages back and forth. In a teen's brain, neurons are still growing and changing and have more "myelination" to go through. To get messages from neuron to neuron, they have to be "louder" or bigger. Because of the more powerful messages sent between the neurons in the teen years, teens experience pleasure and other emotions much more strongly.

" 7 THINGS TO KNOW ABOUT THE TEEN BRAIN

1. The brain reaches its biggest size in early adolescence. For girls, the brain reaches its biggest size around 11 years old. For boys, the brain reaches its biggest size around age 14. But this difference does not mean either boys or girls are smarter than one another!

2. The brain continues to mature even after it is done growing. Though the brain may be done growing in size, it does not finish developing and maturing until the mid-to late 20s. The front part of the brain, called the prefrontal cortex, is one of the last brain regions to mature. This area is responsible for skills like planning, prioritizing, and controlling impulses. Because these skills are still developing, teens are more likely to engage in risky behaviors without considering the potential results of their decisions.

3. The teen brain is ready to learn and adapt. The teen brain has lots of plasticity, which means it can change, adapt, and respond to its environment. Challenging academics or mental activities, exercise, and creative activities such as art can help the brain mature and learn.

4. Many mental disorders may begin to appear during adolescence. Ongoing changes in the brain, along with physical, emotional, and social changes, can make teens vulnerable to mental health problems. All the big changes the brain is experiencing may explain why adolescence is a time when many mental disorders— such as schizophrenia, anxiety, depression, bipolar disorder, and eating disorders—can emerge.

5. Teen brains may be more vulnerable to stress. Because the teen brain is still developing, teens may respond to stress differently than adults, which could lead to stress-related mental disorders such as anxiety and depression. Mindfulness, which is a psychological process of actively paying attention to the present moment, may help teens cope with and reduce stress.

6. Teens need more sleep than children and adults. Research shows that melatonin (the "sleep hormone") levels in the blood are naturally higher later at night and drop later in the morning in teens than in most children and adults. This difference may explain why many teens stay up late and struggle with getting up in the morning. Teens should get about 9 to 10 hours of sleep a night, but most teens do not get enough sleep. A lack of sleep can make it difficult to pay attention, may increase impulsivity, and may increase the risk for irritability or depression.

7. The teen brain is resilient. Although adolescence is a vulnerable time for the brain and for teenagers in general, most teens go on to become healthy adults. Some changes in the brain during this important phase of development actually may help protect against long-term mental disorders.

SOURCE : National Institute on Drug Abuse; National Institutes of Health; U.S. Department of Health and Human Services.

CHAPTER SEVEN

HOW SUBSTANCES HIJACK THE BRAIN

Did you know there's no feeling of happiness or high that can't be produced in a healthy way? Dopamine is the reward chemical produced by your brain that makes you feel good. Endorphins are stress reducing Chemicals produced naturally in the body that ease anxiety and promote a feeling of well-being. Endorphins are released during exercise, and they are a reason so many people enjoy and rely on exercise. We'll talk about Natural Highs later. In this chapter we'll look at the way drugs and alcohol trick the brain and make it so hard to stop using.

How The Brain Is Hijacked

You now understand the way your Brain functions, the time it takes to mature, and the differences between an Adolescent and an Adult Brain. Now, we will show what happens when your brain is tricked by substances and alcohol.

WHAT CHEMICALS
MAKE YOU HIGH?

CAN YOU GET HIGH
NATURALLY?

HOW DO DRUGS
TRICK YOUR BRAIN?

NEURON COMMUNICATION

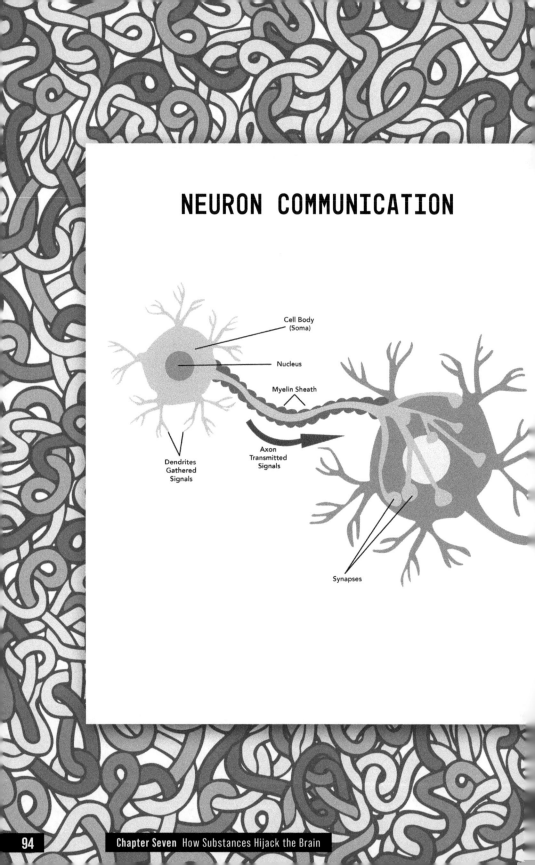

Cell Body (Soma)

Nucleus

Myelin Sheath

Dendrites Gathered Signals

Axon Transmitted Signals

Synapses

HOW DRUGS INTERFERE WITH BRAIN CELLS' COMMUNICATION

When substances reach your brain, the drugs mimic your brain chemicals' shape and size. Your brain cells use your brain chemicals to transfer messages. But drugs and alcohol interfere with this communication system by stopping the transfer of your brain chemicals.

4 FACTS ABOUT TEEN DEVELOPMENT

1. The Prefrontal Lobe is one of the last parts of your brain to develop.

2. Teens' Memories are affected more so than adults' after consuming alcohol, which can lead to more frequent blackouts in adolescents.

3. Adolescents act on their Feelings more than their Logic due to their developed Limbic System overpowering their prefrontal lobe.

4. Teens are also more likely to engage in Risky Behaviors because their prefrontal lobe is still in the process of maturing.

SIX WAYS DRUGS DAMAGE BRAIN FUNCTION

1. Drugs increase your dopamine, or the reward chemicals, which helps you relax, or gives you a high feeling. Because it feels good, the user wants more.

2. After using, dopamine tells your brain and body that you only need the drugs or alcohol. Sleep, food, and relationships become secondary to getting substances into the system.

3. Once drugs are used long-term, the Amygdala, which is where memories and emotions are processed, may start sending your stress-response system into overdrive.

4. Over time, drugs and alcohol can change Brain Function. Your ability to make good judgments, learn, remember, make decisions, and control yourself are impaired.

5. Drugs and alcohol eventually become a necessity and lose their pleasure. The need for drugs is now compulsive and all consuming.

6. The constant use of substances has damaged the Reward Pathways in your brain. You can no longer feel pleasure, happiness, or connections with other people naturally.

YOUR BRAIN ON DRUGS CONTROLS YOUR WHOLE BODY

Your Brain is the control center for your body. That means that 4 body systems are impacted by any substances that are used.

Circulatory System feels the effects from drugs and alcohol by impacting your heart which stops functioning correctly.

- Blood pressure rises.

- Blood vessels can clog, blocking oxygen and nutrients from circulating.

- The heart struggles to work harder.

- This can cause blood clots, stroke, heart attacks, and possibly death.

Respiratory System is affected because drugs cause abnormal lung function.

- Gas exchange is impaired, causing disease-like pneumonia and cancer.

- If drugs are inhaled or smoked, like cocaine and heroin, they deposit on your lungs.

Digestive System Drugs and alcohol damage and breakdown the mucous membranes that line your digestive tract.

- This causes nausea, dehydration, cramps, cancer, ulcers, and constipation.

Endocrine System(glands) is affected in various ways.

- Rise in blood sugar.

- Problems absorbing nutrients which can lead to anemia, digestion problems, skin issues, osteoporosis, and dementia .

- Loss of testosterone, which can lead to low sperm count, impotence, and infertility .

- Loss of estrogen which causes an irregular menstrual cycle or infertility.

WHAT IS ADDICTION

Addiction is a psychological and physical inability to stop consuming a chemical, drug, substance, or participating in a risky activity even though it is causing psychological and physical harm.

What this means, in a nutshell, is that a person can't stop using substances (including tobacco, e cigs, marijuana, amphetamines, alcohol), can't stop eating, can't stop starving, can't stop buying things, exercising, gaming, gambling or any number of other activities even though those things destroy health, relationships, work, or school. To be addicted literally means you can't stop, and if you try to stop, you feel the effects of withdrawal and have to start using or doing the activities again to feel "normal." Your whole life becomes about getting your drug of choice, no matter how much it harms you and others. You can't think about anything else or do anything else.

CHAPTER EIGHT
ALCOHOL & MARIJUANA

According to the World Health Organization, alcohol is still the king of addictions; but marijuana use among teens (and adults) is rising in popularity as more states legalize recreational marijuana use. They may seem innocent enough to try, but using any substances changes brain function at any age and can impact every aspect of life. Delaying experimentation is important because teens are more vulnerable to adverse effects and addiction than adults. Pregnant women avoid alcohol to protect the brains of their unborn babies. Even in the teen years, however, your brain needs the same protection.

There is a dark side to drinking. Alcohol is toxic and addictive and even more dangerous for girls because females process alcohol more quickly than males. In fact, one drink for a boy equals two drinks for a girl. If you don't know the facts, you are at risk for accidents and assault.

HOW DOES MARIJUANA IMPACT A TEEN BRAIN?

WHY DO GIRLS GET DRUNK QUICKER AND STAY DRUNK LONGER?

HOW MANY DRINKS IS IT SAFE FOR A GIRL TO HAVE? IT'S A TRICK QUESTION.

ALCOHOL

Alcohol is a depressant. Drinking looks like such fun in TV shows and the movies, but man's oldest and favorite intoxicant is also a toxin with a dark side, especially for teens and young adults. Did you know that 1 in 4 college students is sexually assaulted as the result of drinking? How does that happen? We'll explain how alcohol affects the brain and body, but first this question:

Why do some people get drunk quicker and stay drunk longer?

The effect alcohol has on your central nervous system (CNS) depends on a variety of factors.

1. Gender: males and females process alcohol differently.

2. The length of time you've been drinking

3. Drinking on an empty stomach

4. Mixing alcohol with energy drinks or other drugs

5. How often and how much you drink

6. Genetics and ethnic background

7. Size and weight

GIRLS VS. BOYS

People tend to think that when girls get drunk, they know what they are doing. In fact, most people don't know that alcohol is twice as potent for girls. One drink for a boy has the impact of two drinks in a girl. That means a girl who has three drinks will experience the effects of six drinks. She'll be incapacitated, may vomit and pass out, while the boys she's drinking with are still rocking and rolling.

Why are girls so vulnerable to alcohol?

Boys have about 10% more water in their bodies than girls which dilutes alcohol as it circulates. Boys are taller, heavier, and have more muscle (muscle has more water than fat).

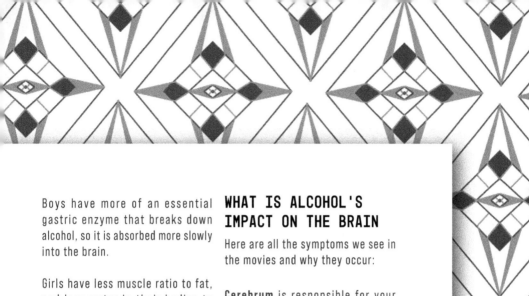

Boys have more of an essential gastric enzyme that breaks down alcohol, so it is absorbed more slowly into the brain.

Girls have less muscle ratio to fat, and less water in their bodies to dilute alcohol as it circulates in the body.

Girls produce less of the gastric enzyme needed to slow alcohol's absorption into the brain.

Women absorb 30% more alcohol into their blood than men of equal proportions who drink the same amount. This causes women to have higher blood alcohol content.

When girls skip meals prior to drinking they will feel the effects even more.

In short, girls get drunk quicker and stay drunk longer

WHAT IS ALCOHOL'S IMPACT ON THE BRAIN

Here are all the symptoms we see in the movies and why they occur:

Cerebrum is responsible for your movements. Alcohol decreases your ability to think clearly. Blurs vision, slurs speech, impairs hearing, slows your reaction time, and throws off your balance and coordination.

Medulla controls your breathing and the maintenance of body temperature. Alcohol consumption can shut down the medulla and lead to blackouts and coma.

Hypothalamus controls your heart rate, thirst, and hunger. Alcohol slows your heart, and you become thirsty. Alcohol is a diuretic, which means it causes you to expel a lot of liquid. You can become dehydrated.

Hippocampus is where your memories live. When drinking, your memories are compromised. After long-term, excessive drinking, this area can become permanently damaged, which prevents you from retaining new information.

ALCOHOL'S EFFECT ON BEHAVIOR

Alcohol is a toxin in every way, and nowhere is that fact revealed more than in your behavior when you drink. Your values, your sense of self, your caring for others, and your ability to be responsible can all go out the window with a drink or two. Here's what happens even to the very best people.

Alcohol lowers inhibitions, so you feel it's all right to do things you would never do sober. This happens to adults, too.

Impacts your senses; bad situations that should send off alarm bells are disguised by alcohol as fun.

You can forget who you are and what you believe.

You lose emotional control and act wild and crazy: mad, sad, or violent which can lead to accidents, assaults, legal problems, and a lifetime of guilt. You lose the ability to make healthy decisions.

You want to drink more instead of stopping to protect yourself from harming yourself and others.

You take dares and engage in risky activities that can hurt you and others.

Underage drinking leads to smoking and experimenting with other substances, even heroin.

Then there's the aftermath of just one bad night. You can feel shame and hurt for the rest of your life for something that happened while you were drinking as a teen.

ALCOHOL'S EFFECT ON THE BODY

Alcohol is a toxin in other ways. Advertising encourages us to think of alcohol as a major part of the human party. It's true that alcohol has been around since the beginning of time. We can't blame our current society for creating an alcohol-loving world, but this is what most people don't know. Alcohol can hurt you in many ways not just in the teen years but over the course of many years.

Brain: Binge drinking in teens, and heavy drinking over time create brain impairment and brain damage, permanently affecting memory, behavior, and motor skills.

Heart: Blood pressure increases, heart rate increases: Your heart can beat abnormally and may increase the size of your heart.

Stomach: Your stomach gets upset. When you drink too much, nausea and vomiting result. Alcohol also impairs food digestion and the ability to make necessary proteins. Heavy drinking causes malnutrition and over time and can cause ulcers, bleeding, and cancer of the stomach or colon.

Liver: Alcohol weakens the liver, making it difficult to filter the blood and keep it toxin-free. Heavy drinking leads to liver diseases such as hepatitis, cirrhosis, and cancer.

Reproductive organs: Over time alcohol can affect sexual performance in men. Heavy drinking can affect reproduction in women, and women can experience painful, irregular periods.

Babies: Women who drink even moderately while pregnant risk having children with Fetal Alcohol Syndrome.

Mouth, throat, breast, bowel, esophagus, and pancreas cancer risks are increased by regular heavy alcohol consumption.

Heavy drinkers may also experience weight gain due to the increased calorie intake.

MARIJUANA

Marijuana is a depressant, stimulant, and hallucinogen. That means a variety of effects can occur. With the legalization of marijuana in many states and the rise of the medical marijuana business, some people believe marijuana is safe to use. Since not enough research has been done to validate the hype, however, the jury is still out on the benefits of medical marijuana.

It's important to note that new products are always highly praised. When heroin, tobacco, cocaine, and amphetamines were introduced, they too were touted as totally safe cure-alls. What is well-researched is the damage that marijuana use can do to young brains. Here are the facts.

The Cannabis plant, from which Marijuana is derived, has over 400 chemicals. Sixty of those chemicals are cannabinoids. The main ingredient in marijuana is Tetrahydrocannabinol (THC). THC is what makes your brain cells release dopamine, the brain's reward chemical. Dopamine occurs naturally, but when released by a drug like marijuana, the result is a combination of unnatural highs and brain changes that vary greatly depending on the person using it.

Because of its complex chemical makeup, marijuana can have surprising and opposing effects, and there is no way to tell whether marijuana use will affect you as a depressant, stimulant, hallucinogen or combination of the three. Cannabis is the most widely-used illicit drug in the world, and its use has been associated with various mental health problems, particularly in the young.

HOW DOES MARIJUANA AFFECT THE BRAIN

THC gets to the brain quickly when marijuana is smoked.

THC prevents the system from working properly, throwing it off balance by hijacking what are called cannabinoid receptors in the brain and slowing down the connection and communication between cells.

TCH can affect your behavior in many ways.

THC remains in the body for a minimum of 30 days, usually in the brain, testes, ovaries, and fatty organs.

HOW DOES MARIJUANA AFFECT THE BRAIN

Brain: Long-term use changes brain function affecting brain development and decreasing IQ.

Cerebellum: Marijuana impairs function by slowing reactions and motor skills, making it dangerous to drive and participate in sports.

Hippocampus: Marijuana use impairs memory making it more difficult to remember things and complete tasks. Hypothalamus: Marijuana stimulates appetite which can lead to weight gain and complications from added weight.

Lungs: Smoking marijuana irritates the lungs producing symptoms of coughing, wheezing, asthma, bronchitis, and shortness of breath.

Heart: Marijuana increases blood pressure and heart rate. Over time, it could have opposite effects, causing low blood pressure or heart rate.

Reproductive Organs: Marijuana use decreases testosterone production, sperm counts, and sperm mobility in males. May lead to impotence. In women, menstrual cycles become irregular, builds prolactin levels leading to milk secretion when not breastfeeding.

Spinal Cord: Alters sensitivity to pain through the spinal cord. Marijuana is a complicated drug that affects people in different ways. Smoking pot can stimulate the appetite and distort the senses. Users see and hear things that aren't there. The experience of intense sensations can be frightening and cause unexpected reactions for those with emotional vulnerabilities or mental illness.

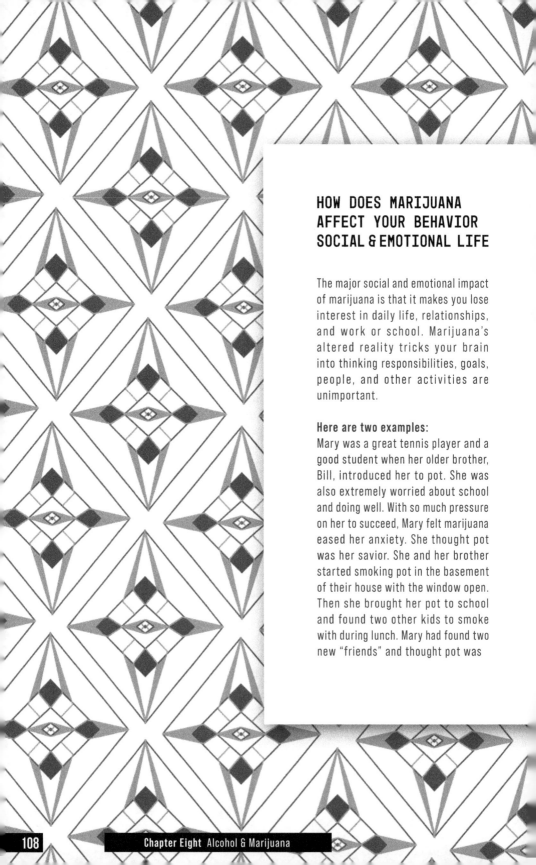

HOW DOES MARIJUANA AFFECT YOUR BEHAVIOR SOCIAL & EMOTIONAL LIFE

The major social and emotional impact of marijuana is that it makes you lose interest in daily life, relationships, and work or school. Marijuana's altered reality tricks your brain into thinking responsibilities, goals, people, and other activities are unimportant.

Here are two examples:
Mary was a great tennis player and a good student when her older brother, Bill, introduced her to pot. She was also extremely worried about school and doing well. With so much pressure on her to succeed, Mary felt marijuana eased her anxiety. She thought pot was her savior. She and her brother started smoking pot in the basement of their house with the window open. Then she brought her pot to school and found two other kids to smoke with during lunch. Mary had found two new "friends" and thought pot was

improving her life. In fact, she was hiding, sneaking, lying to her parents and teachers, and performing poorly in class. Tennis became a burden she didn't want to carry. In a period of six months, Mary's behavior had changed. What should her parents and teachers do to help her?

Dan was a bright kid, but more interested in his social life than his studies. Dan started smoking because pot was around his school, and it didn't seem to be a big deal. Other students told him pot was safer than alcohol. Smoking pot made Dan feel part of a group he admired. It gave them something to do together. This group also used alcohol and other substances. Dan became caught up in a life that encouraged more risky behaviors and alienated him from his parents who now had trouble reaching him.

THE EMOTIONAL & SOCIAL IMPACT OF REGULAR MARIJUANA USE

Loss of interest in life and goals

Unable to focus in school

Less satisfaction with life

Neglect of social events, school, and activities

Increased risk of anxiety and depression.

When used frequently, marijuana can be linked to high dropout rates, poor grades, and more accidents behind the wheel of cars, bikes, and other vehicles. Marijuana can be addictive when used regularly; teens who use the drug are more likely to experiment with other drugs. That is the reason marijuana is often referred to as the gateway drug. Those who are addicted to marijuana are three times more likely to become addicted to heroin.

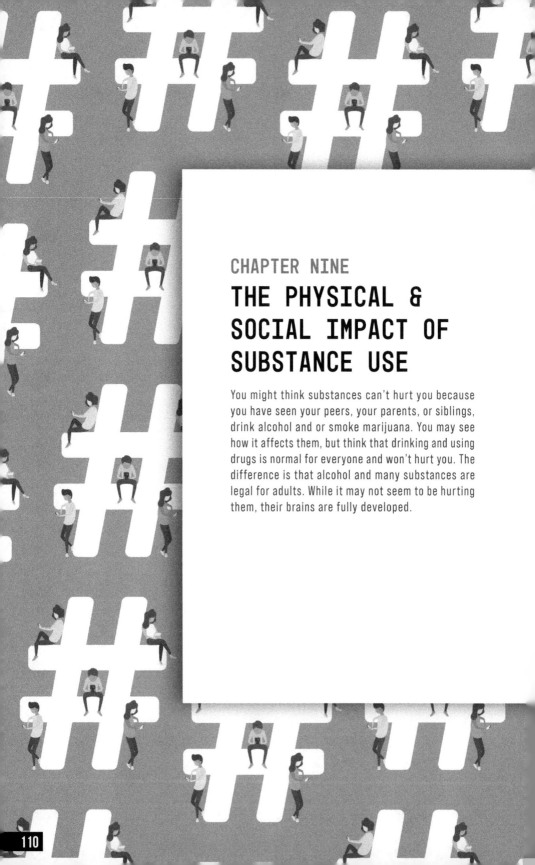

CHAPTER NINE

THE PHYSICAL & SOCIAL IMPACT OF SUBSTANCE USE

You might think substances can't hurt you because you have seen your peers, your parents, or siblings, drink alcohol and or smoke marijuana. You may see how it affects them, but think that drinking and using drugs is normal for everyone and won't hurt you. The difference is that alcohol and many substances are legal for adults. While it may not seem to be hurting them, their brains are fully developed.

Teen use may also seem normal. Do you think every teen has gotten drunk and had fun with no ill effects? You have seen the "fun" side in movies, and you have seen negative consequences in those movies, too. It may be difficult, however, to imagine that you could get seriously hurt just by drinking with friends or taking a few pills. Yet, as we have said earlier, some 15% of high school students do become addicted and have negative consequences. This chapter explores the physical and social impact of substance use.

HAVE ANY OF YOUR FRIENDS BEEN HURT BY DRUGS?

ARE DRINKING AND MARIJUANA SAFE?

HOW MANY TEENS ARE ADDICTED?

SOCIAL IMPACT OF SUBSTANCE USE

Intoxicants (which include legal and illegal substances) affect your life in every way. They can hinder you physically, mentally, emotionally, and socially. But how do they affect your relationships? Your friendships? Your future? Here are two examples.

High school softball player, Jessica has started experimenting with drugs. All of her friends are on the team and stay away from substances to ensure they won't be forced to leave. Jessica isn't too worried, so she continues using— the drugs help her to relax. Her friends are fine with it in the beginning. Or, they say they are.

But slowly, Jessica develops a tolerance to substances and needs more to get the same feeling. She starts getting sick when she doesn't have her drug of choice and uses just to feel normal. She falls out of the loop. She hasn't been to the park with her friends in weeks, and she's no longer involved in her group chats. After a while, Jessica has lost interest and is no longer on the softball team. She's either alone or hanging out with a different crowd that shares her substance addiction.

HOW SUBSTANCE USE CHANGED JESSICA'S SOCIAL LIFE

- Jessica is the only one in her group who is regularly using drugs. Her friends are wary of her decision and don't want to be involved in something that can get them kicked off the team or hurt their chances for scholarships and college.

- Jessica's mood changes drastically. Whether she is high or waiting for her next fix, her moods change rapidly and without warning. Her friends are nervous around her because she is unpredictable.

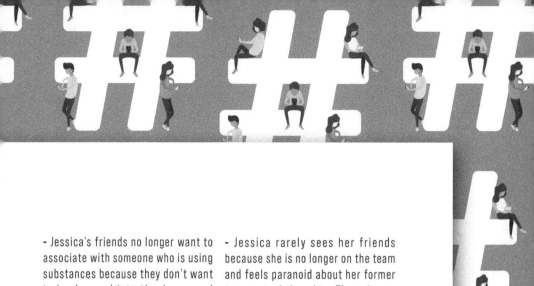

- Jessica's friends no longer want to associate with someone who is using substances because they don't want to be dragged into the drama and the danger.

- Her friends have caught her lying, shoplifting, and stealing from her parents to get money for drugs.

- Jessica slowly begins using more and more, which leads her to isolate herself. Since her friends don't accept her actions while high, she hides her abuse from them.

- Her friends especially don't appreciate her: Lies, Stealing,Other Crimes that may be committed to obtain drugs.

- Jessica is released from the softball team because she rarely shows up for practice and her performance as an athlete declined.

- Jessica rarely sees her friends because she is no longer on the team and feels paranoid about her former teammates' thoughts. They also no longer keep her in the loop or contact her to go out.

- Her grades drop because she is no longer interested in getting good grades and can no longer focus in class.

- She has changed. Her judgment is impaired. She now joins a new group of friends in risky behaviors.

- Jessica is no longer working to apply to college because without a softball scholarship, she will have a difficult time paying for the tuition. Her grades are low, and she feels that she will never be accepted into higher education now.

HOW SUBSTANCE USE AFFECTED CHARLIE'S PHYSICAL LIFE

Jessica's cousin Charlie also uses drugs. However, he says he "only uses at parties." In fact, he has developed a taste for alcohol and marijuana and sometimes other harder drugs. He now uses them on his own whenever he "needs to relax." He has hopes of one day becoming a famous actor and singer. Charlie has just landed a starring role in his high school's musical and is celebrating with friends. However, while his cast members stayed sober, he continued using. His classmates become worried.

Physically, Charlie's body begins to feel the effects of the drugs and alcohol. He is having a difficult time learning and retaining all of the stage directions, dances, and his lines. His cast members are growing impatient with him, and he can't help but feel aggressive towards them. He misses rehearsals due to feeling too sick or too high and he's falling behind in both the musical and his schoolwork.

Charlie's brain, lungs, heart, mouth, glands, liver, stomach, intestines, and kidneys all suffer from the stress of substance use. He has lost a lot of weight between the beginning of the year and opening night due to the drugs' suppressing his appetite and hijacking his brain to claim high importance. Other effects from his drug use include:

- Disturbed sleep patterns. Many drugs alter sleep patterns and cause insomnia. Due to lack of sleep, Charlie has trouble concentrating the next day and has memory issues.

- Charlie's moods have become unpredictable as well, leading him to have outbursts in the middle of his rehearsals.

- Drugs affect brain growth, which hinder Charlie's ability to learn and retain his lines and other important information. He suffers from memory loss and, if his habit continues, can eventually suffer brain damage. The lack of oxygen from his slowed breathing hurts his brain.

- Charlie's lungs' strength and flexibility slowly decline. They are impacted due to snorting and inhaling substances. He can no longer hold a note or project his voice as well as he once could without gasping for air. If he continues his use, he can develop lung cancer, emphysema, respiratory failure, and other lung diseases.

- Charlie can't dance without having to stop because his muscles are too tired and weak. The lack of blood, oxygen, and poor circulation have made it that much more difficult for him to perform the lengthy numbers and difficult choreography. His poor attendance at rehearsals makes it difficult for him to develop the necessary stamina.

- His substance use can lead to heart attack, stroke, constricted vessels, collapsed veins, and infections to his heart and blood vessels.

- Charlie often feels queasy and tends to have pains in his abdominal area. He sometimes finds himself in the bathroom during and after rehearsals, wondering if he will vomit or if he will fight off the wave of nausea.

- His singing voice also suffers due to the burning from acid reflux and smoke inhalation. He struggles to hit the higher notes he used to sing with ease.

- His stomach and intestines can become damaged or develop cancer and bowel tissue decay.

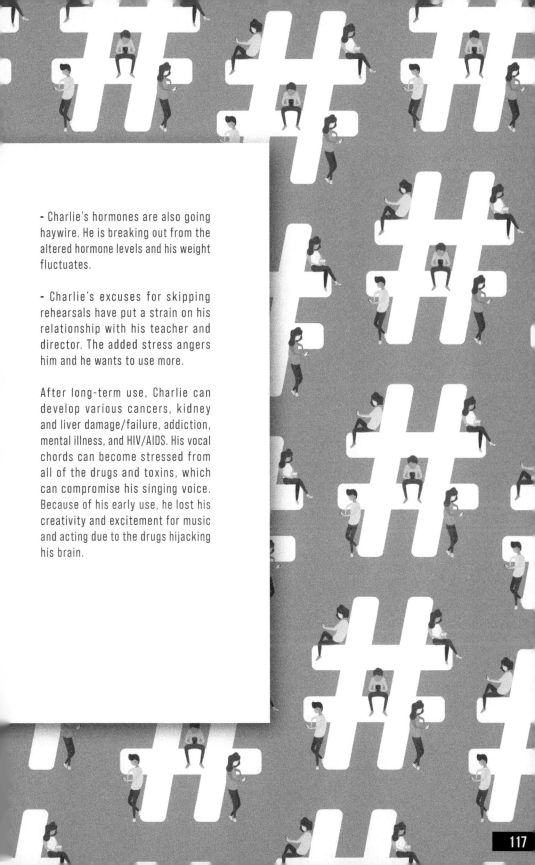

- Charlie's hormones are also going haywire. He is breaking out from the altered hormone levels and his weight fluctuates.

- Charlie's excuses for skipping rehearsals have put a strain on his relationship with his teacher and director. The added stress angers him and he wants to use more.

After long-term use, Charlie can develop various cancers, kidney and liver damage/failure, addiction, mental illness, and HIV/AIDS. His vocal chords can become stressed from all of the drugs and toxins, which can compromise his singing voice. Because of his early use, he lost his creativity and excitement for music and acting due to the drugs hijacking his brain.

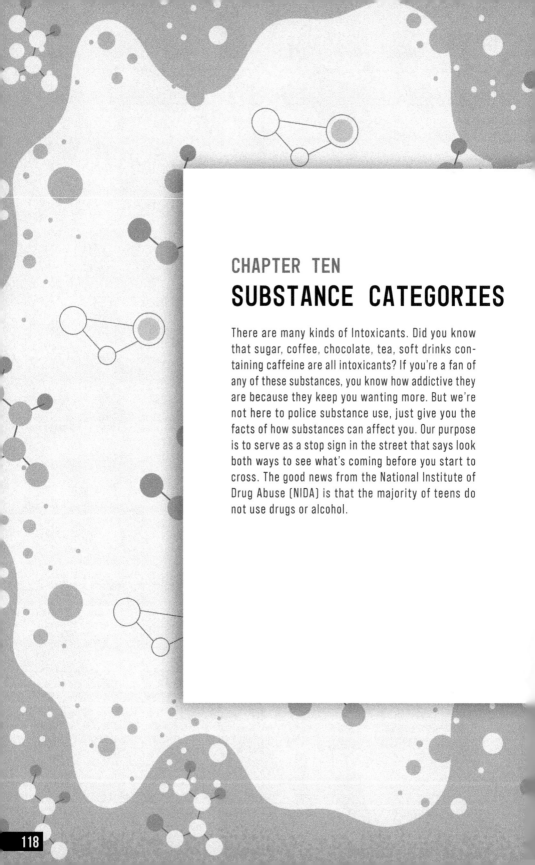

CHAPTER TEN
SUBSTANCE CATEGORIES

There are many kinds of Intoxicants. Did you know that sugar, coffee, chocolate, tea, soft drinks containing caffeine are all intoxicants? If you're a fan of any of these substances, you know how addictive they are because they keep you wanting more. But we're not here to police substance use, just give you the facts of how substances can affect you. Our purpose is to serve as a stop sign in the street that says look both ways to see what's coming before you start to cross. The good news from the National Institute of Drug Abuse (NIDA) is that the majority of teens do not use drugs or alcohol.

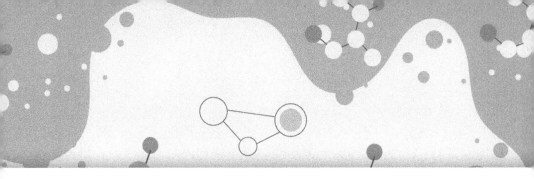

What are the different kinds of drugs?

1. Stimulants

2. Depressants

3. Hallucinogens

WHAT ARE INTOXICANTS?

ARE ALL INTOXICANTS
ADDICTIVE?

THE MAJORITY OF TEENS
DO/DON'T USE DRUGS?

WHAT ARE THE DIFFERENT KINDS OF DRUGS

The three main categories of drugs and alcohol are: **Stimulants, Depressants**, and **Hallucinogens.**

1. Stimulants, also known as "uppers," send the user's body and brain into hyperactivity, super alertness. Two examples of stimulants are Cocaine and Amphetamines. Stimulants can be taken a number of ways including swallowing, injecting, and snorting.

2.Depressants, also called "downers," slow the body and brain down. Depressants include Tranquilizers, Antipsychotics, Sleeping Pills, Heroin, Opioids, Marijuana, and Alcohol.

3. Hallucinogens are drugs that cause profound distortions in a person's perceptions of reality. They are commonly split into two categories: classic hallucinogens (such as LSD) and Dissociative Drugs (such as PCP). Under the influence of hallucinogens, people see images, hear sounds, and feel sensations that seem real but do not exist. Some hallucinogens also produce rapid, intense emotional swings.

THE DANGER OF MIXING DRUGS ALCOHOL & ENERGY DRINKS

Drugs and alcohol each take their toll on the human body when used alone, but when mixed they are dangerous and unpredictable. Most of the fatal overdoses are caused by mixing two or more drugs. Even mixing energy drinks (caffeine) with alcohol can cause a heart attack in a healthy teen. Mixing Depressants with Stimulants, for example, sends opposing messages to your Organs and intensifies harmful effects that can lead to heart attacks, seizures, comas, violent acts, memory loss, and death.

OTHER PEOPLE'S MEDICINE CABINETS

Sometimes people sell or share their Medications or take them from other people's medicine cabinets. It is tempting to think that medicines prescribed by doctors are safe for everyone. But that is not true. When you take medicines prescribed to balance someone else's body or brain, you could unbalance your own brain or body. Pain medicines for a friend or relative, for example, are for their physical or psychological needs. Your body could have a bad reaction. Adderall, for example, is prescribed for ADHD. It helps that disorder. As we have shown, medications are substances that can be helpful, or addictive and harmful. When they are taken by someone who is not suffering from a physical or mental ailment, or misused, they can have lasting damaging effects.

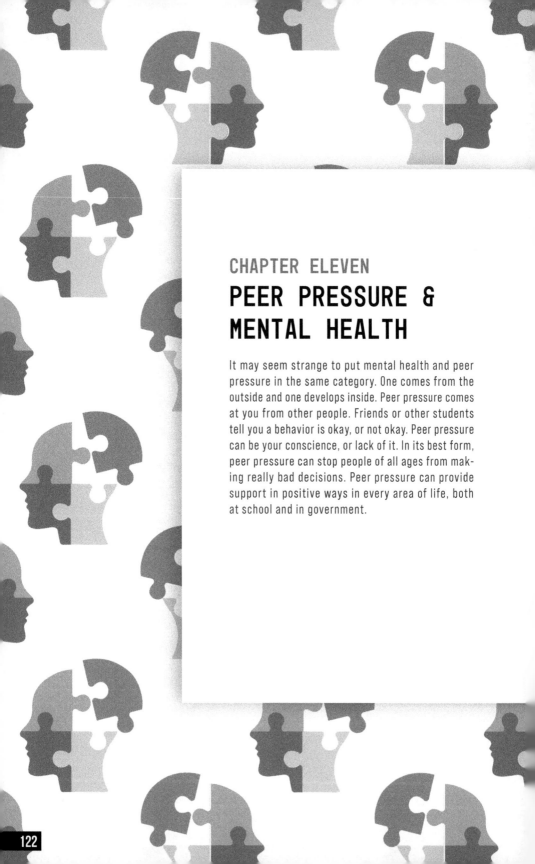

CHAPTER ELEVEN
PEER PRESSURE & MENTAL HEALTH

It may seem strange to put mental health and peer pressure in the same category. One comes from the outside and one develops inside. Peer pressure comes at you from other people. Friends or other students tell you a behavior is okay, or not okay. Peer pressure can be your conscience, or lack of it. In its best form, peer pressure can stop people of all ages from making really bad decisions. Peer pressure can provide support in positive ways in every area of life, both at school and in government.

Peer pressure can promote healthy choices and behaviors and push back against bullying and other forms of abuse. On the other hand, peer pressure that promotes hatred or fear, risky and dangerous behaviors is unhealthy for you and everyone else. Bullying and abuse also come from outside of you and are perpetrated by other people.

HOW ARE YOU AFFECTED BY PEER PRESSURE?

CAN PEER PRESSURE BE USED IN A HEALTHY WAY?

NAME A HEALTHY PEER PRESSURE?

WHAT DOES MENTAL HEALTH HAVE TO DO WITH PEER PRESSURE

Mental Health has to do with everything. Your mental health empowers you to use your critical thinking to make healthy decisions, no matter what is happening around you. Your mental health gives you the power to survive abuse, adverse experiences at home or in your community. It is like a shield that can provide the armor you need to resist the temptations of negative peer pressure. It is the very core of your being.

Your mental health is the voice that tells you to be strong when you're hurting and afraid. It is the tool that helps you calm down when anxiety keeps you up at night. It is the investigator that looks for help, answers, and solutions from safe people. There is always something you can do, someone you can turn to. And your mental health is what guides you and protects you from making poor decisions.

Mental health is the combination of all the factors we've been exploring: your physical health, your emotional health, and your social health. All three contribute to your mental health. You need all three working together to be healthy.

WHAT ARE THE KINDS OF MENTAL ILLNESS

You may wonder what is Mental Illness. Where does it come from? Do I have it? Does someone in my family have it? What will happen to me if I do have it? The list below comes from the National Alliance of Mental Health (NAMI) and describes the kinds of mental illness that require treatment.

You may be familiar with, or have heard about, some or all of them. Mental illness can run in your family, just as alcoholism and substance addiction, but that doesn't mean

that you have it or will get it. Mental illness has a history of being stigmatized, but as awareness about it grows and we recognize how common it is. Acceptance and treatment is improving as well.

We all have some symptoms of one or more of these disorders. Who isn't anxious or depressed sometimes, for example? Most of us have experienced trauma and depression. Your mental health can be disrupted in a number of ways. Drinking alcohol and using substances can trigger symptoms of mental illness described below with lasting effects to your brain and behavior. Over time and with treatment, the brain can heal. See Teen Health and Substances.

Anxiety may be the most common symptom we all feel sometimes. Everyone can experience anxiety, but when symptoms are overwhelming and constant — often impacting everyday living — it may be an anxiety disorder.

Attention Deficit Hyperactivity Disorder ADHD is a developmental disorder defined by inattention (trouble staying on task, listening); disorganization (losing materials); and hyperactivity-impulsivity (fidgeting, difficulty staying seated or waiting).

Bipolar Disorder causes dramatic shifts in a person's mood, energy and ability to think clearly. Individuals with this disorder experience extreme high and low moods, known as mania and depression. Some people can be symptom-free for many years between episodes.

Borderline Personality Disorder is characterized by a pattern of instability in emotions interpersonal relationships and self-image. Individuals with BPD can also struggle with impulsivity and self-harm.

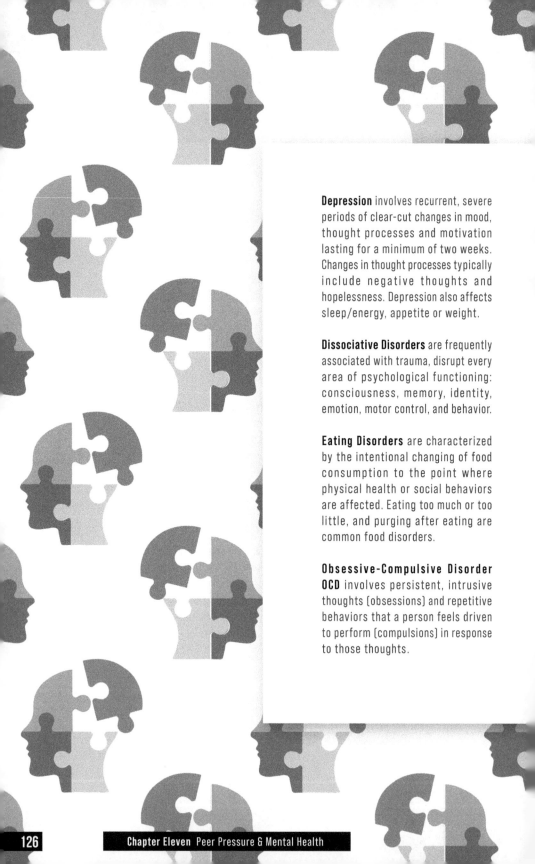

Depression involves recurrent, severe periods of clear-cut changes in mood, thought processes and motivation lasting for a minimum of two weeks. Changes in thought processes typically include negative thoughts and hopelessness. Depression also affects sleep/energy, appetite or weight.

Dissociative Disorders are frequently associated with trauma, disrupt every area of psychological functioning: consciousness, memory, identity, emotion, motor control, and behavior.

Eating Disorders are characterized by the intentional changing of food consumption to the point where physical health or social behaviors are affected. Eating too much or too little, and purging after eating are common food disorders.

Obsessive-Compulsive Disorder OCD involves persistent, intrusive thoughts (obsessions) and repetitive behaviors that a person feels driven to perform (compulsions) in response to those thoughts.

Post Traumatic Stress Disorder PTSD involves a set of physiological and psychological responses. It can occur in people who have experienced or witnessed a traumatic event such as a natural disaster, a serious accident, a terrorist act, rape, war/combat or systematic family abuse.

Psychosis is characterized as disruptions to a person's thoughts and perceptions that make it difficult for them to recognize what is real and what isn't.

Schizoaffective Disorder involves symptoms of schizophrenia, such as hallucinations or delusions, and symptoms of a mood disorder, such as depressive or manic episodes.

Schizophrenia interferes with a person's ability to think clearly, manage emotions, make decisions, and relate to others. It also causes people to lose touch with reality in the form of hallucinations and delusions.

WHAT ABOUT PHYSICAL PAIN & ANXIETY

Everyone feels Pain and Anxiety. No one is happy all the time. And no one has a totally pain-free life. From the day we're born we all have injuries and illnesses that cause physical pain.

Pain Management is in the news because addictive medicines, like opioids, have commonly been prescribed unnecessarily. Further, we tend to think as a culture that physical pain can be lessened with medicine. Research has shown in the last 20 years, however, that people have been using more powerful (and addictive) pain medications than they need. Most pain can be managed with over-the-counter analgesics like Aspirin, Tylenol, and Aleve. The body does tend to heal itself.

" DO I HAVE DEPRESSION

- Do you often feel sad, anxious, worthless, or even "empty"?

- Have you lost interest in activities you used to enjoy?

- Do you get easily frustrated, irritable, or angry?

- Do you find yourself withdrawing from friends and family?

- Are your grades dropping?

- Have your eating or sleeping habits changed?

- Have you experienced any fatigue or memory loss?

- Have you thought about suicide or harming yourself?

Depression looks different for everyone. You might have many of the symptoms listed above or just a few.

HOW DO I GET HELP FOR DEPRESSION

You're not alone, and help is available. You can feel better. To get help:

- **Talk to a trusted adult** (such as your parent or guardian, teacher, or school counselor) about how you've been feeling.

- **Ask your doctor** about options for professional help. Depression can be treated with psychotherapy (also called "talk therapy"), medication, or a combination of medication and talk therapy.

- **Try to spend time with friends or family,** even if you don't feel like you want to.

- **Stay active and exercise**, even if it's just going for a walk. Physical activity releases chemicals, such as endorphins, in your brain that can help you feel better.

- **Try to keep a regular sleep schedule.**

- **Eat healthy foods.**

SOURCE: National Institute on Drug Abuse; National Institutes of Health; U.S. Department of Health and Human Services.

WHAT CAN YOU DO ABOUT EMOTIONAL PAIN AND ANXIETY

We've either been hurt by others, or we're going to get hurt emotionally by events and by people at some time in our lives. Bullying is only one way we can feel powerless and hurt. Getting hurt and feeling hurt, as well as feeling anxiety, are part of the human experience. Learning to manage our pain and anxiety are part of growing up. While the body may heal, anxiety doesn't fade away by itself. Neither do the stress and pain from emotional abuse fade away.

Emotional Pain and anxiety are two common reasons teens and adults seek to numb their feelings with alcohol or other substances. While using drugs can get you off a healthy path for your life, no one gets better or does better from using them.

5 TIPS FOR DEALING WITH EMOTIONAL PAIN & ANXIETY

1. Tell someone you trust If you are being hurt either physically or emotionally, try make it stop. No one is more important than you. Tell a teacher, a policeman, a school counselor, a trusted family member. You may feel powerless, but you are not alone. We know brave children and teens who have had a family member arrested. It isn't the end of the world, but the end of the abuse. We have to note here that It is not always safe to tell, so it's important to know when and how to speak out. You may need protection. Check the resources page at the end of this book for help.

2. Express your feelings and fears If you are overwhelmed, or sad, or lonely or frightened, talk about it to someone who can listen. We all feel this way sometimes. Don't bury your feelings because, honestly, getting them out can help you heal. Be sure to find someone who is safe to tell, someone who can give you advice or support. Again, if it is not safe to speak right now, you can express your feelings in other ways to get relief.

3. Express yourself in a hobby or sport Find something you love to do. Everyone loves something. This may be a sport, or a form of artistic expression. It may be taking care of a sibling or family member who needs you. You can paint, sing, act, sew, get involved with science or nature or animals. You can help by volunteering. There are thousands of ways to express yourself in creative and healing ways.

4. Connect with safe groups in safe places There are groups for teens living with substance use. One of them is Al-Anon.org. Don't feel that you have to keep a dark family secret, or that you don't have the right to connect with other people experiencing the same things you are.

5. Try meditating or yoga Meditation is a way of calming down and recharging your brain and letting go. It can serve as a cleanse of painful thoughts and distractions that keep you unbalanced. Yoga serves as both exercise and strength training and a technique for training your brain.

CHAPTER TWELVE
NATURAL HIGHS

A word about Dopamine. We mentioned earlier that there's no feeling of Wellbeing or Euphoria, Relaxation, Happiness or Contentment that you can't get naturally. This is the irony of drugs and alcohol. By flooding you brain with short blasts dopamine that only serve to make you want more, drugs and alcohol steal your power to feel good on your own. We've talked about all the ways that Stimulants, Depressants, and Hallucinogens can interfere with your brain and body systems. But the most important interference is with your ability to function well, have healthy relationships, and enjoy your life.

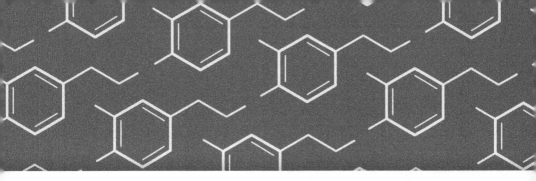

5 ways to get a natural high

1. Exercise

2. Self-Expression

3. Working on a project

4. Accomplishing tasks

5. Being in nature

WHAT IS A NATURAL HIGH?

HOW MANY WAYS CAN YOU GET A NATURAL HIGH?

IS THERE ANY DRUG THAT CAN REPLACE A NATURAL HIGH?

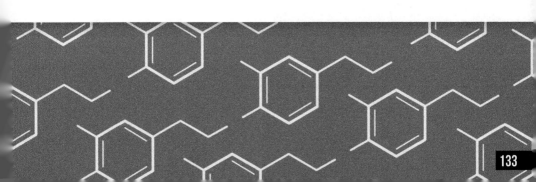

5 WAYS TO GET NATURAL HIGHS

1. Exercise any kind will make you feel good. Walking, running, biking, playing sports, lifting weights, practicing yoga all produce a feeling of wellbeing.

2. Self-Expression in all the ways we talked about before. Sing, dance, laugh, play an instrument, paint a picture, work with wood or stone or clay or glass. Knit a sweater, string beads. Cook, write, plant a garden or just one plant. Take care of loved ones. Anything you do that gives you pleasure is a form of self-expression.

3. Working on a project, problem solving, working with others, doing service for people in need, helping someone who's been hurt or experiencing problems, volunteering, taking care of animals.

4. Accomplishing tasks is a great way to feel good. Whether school work, or a job, or tasks at home, finishing your work and getting something done always provides a good feeling.

5. Being in nature Getting outside allows you to calm down by looking beyond yourself. You can follow the stars, hike on a trail, see animals, watch the clouds and storms, enjoy the sun, and just connect with the natural world.

There are literally thousands of ways to get natural highs, as many ways as there are people with passions. As long as you are connected to something you enjoy, or doing something that provides relief when it's done then you are getting a natural high.

4 QUESTIONS TO ASK YOURSELF ABOUT YOUR NATURAL HIGHS

1. What is my favorite hobby?

2. What is my favorite thing to do with friends or family?

3. What do I like to do outside?

4. What are three new things I could explore to find more natural highs?

Sections of this book use information from these sources:

NAMI National Alliance of Mental Illness

NIDA National Institute of Drug Abuse

NIMH National Institute of Mental Health

NIH National Institute of Health

Harvard's Women's Health Watch

Some images sourced from:

Freepik.com

Resources:

- Center for Young Women's Health and Young Men's Health: These websites provide a series of guides on emotional health, including test anxiety, depression, bullying, and eating disorders. www.youngwomenshealth.org and www.youngmenshealthsite.org

- Go Ask Alice!: Geared at young adults, this question and answer website contains a large database of questions about a variety of concerns surrounding emotional health. www.goaskalice.columbia.edu

- Girls Health.Gov: The "Your Feelings" section of this website offers guidance to teenage girls on recognizing a mental health problem, getting help, and talking to parents. http://girlshealth.gov/feelings/index.html

ABOUT THE AUTHOR

Leslie Glass is founder of the popular recovery website ReachOutRecovery. com with her daughter Lindsey, where the mother/daughter writing team create engaging articles, books, videos, and tools to support healthy living. In addition to her work at Reach Out Recovery, Leslie is a frequent Podcast and Rotary International speaker on Teen Mental Health, Your Family Tree of Mental Health, and Family Recovery from Addiction. Leslie also writes about Recovery and Business for Newsweek as a member of the Newsweek Expert Panel.

An award-winning journalist, filmmaker, author, and recovery advocate. Glass is the USA Today and NY Times bestselling author of 13 novels including nine crime novels featuring Sgt. Det. April Woo the first female Chinese Law Enforcement Officer in mainstream American fiction. After coping with her children's substance and alcohol use in their teen years, Glass decided to use her writing talents for addiction prevention education and to make a difference for other families impacted by mental illness and the family disease of addiction. 2021 marked the ten-year anniversary of the mother/ daughter recovery advocacy and writing team.

Glass received the 2016 American Society of Addiction Medicine (ASAM) Media Award for her and Lindsey's documentary The Secret World of Recovery. The Glass team's documentary The Silent Majority was distributed to all PBS stations in 2015. Her website Reach Out Recovery has attracted more than 5 million visitors since its launch in 2014. Reach Out Recovery posts and videos on social media have 1.5 million monthly views. In addition to The Teen Guide to Health, Glass is the author of recovery workbooks for all ages.

In 2021, Glass used Reach Out Recovery's platform to launch its first high school Art/Media contest, sponsored by Rotary Club of Sarasota Bay which was open to all high school students in Florida's Rotary District 6960. Referencing subjects in The Teen Guide to Health, students created positive mental health messaging through posters, TikTok and YouTube videos, photographs, and paintings to answer the question "What Makes You Healthy?" In 2021 six Art/ Media contest winners were awarded $7850 in scholarships. This teen mental health initiative is a first for Rotary US, providing a both a simple resource supplement for teachers and counselors and scholarship opportunity for high school students. Contest runs from January to July with winners announced after Labor Day. Contests for schools in other areas are in development.

MENTAL HEALTH
RESOURCE INSTITUTES

- **American Academy of Child and Adolescent Psychiatry:** This resource center includes videos, ways to get help, and advocacy campaigns. *aacap.org/*

- **National Alliance on Mental Health:** Find resources for youth, including information on managing your mental health in college and making friends. *nami.org/Find-Support/Teens-and-Young-Adults*

- **National Institute of Mental Health:** This website provides easy-to-read guides and brochures to help better understand a variety of mental health disorders. *nimh.nih.gov/health*

- **Substance Abuse and Mental Health Services Administration:** SAMHSA provides information on mental health services and treatment centers through a service locator. *findtreatment.samhsa.gov/*

- **Making Healthy Choices:** This guide provides information for youth in foster care related to making decisions about their mental health, treatment options, and the use of psychotropic medications. *childwelfare.gov/pubs/makinghealthychoices/*

- **National Eating Disorder Association:** Visit *nationaleatingdisorders.org/* or call *1-800-931-2237*

- **National Suicide Prevention Lifeline:** Visit *suicidepreventionlifeline.org/* or call *1-800-273-TALK (8255)*

- **Active Minds:** The leading nonprofit that empowers college students to speak openly about mental health, Active Minds aims to educate others and encourage help-seeking. *activeminds.org/*

- **Gay, Lesbian & Straight Education Network:** GLSEN is the leading national education organization focused on ensuring safe schools for all students. This website provides resources on finding GSA Chapters, and tools on how to establish or re-establish a GSA. *www.glsen.org*

- The trevor project : The Trevor Project is the world's largest suicide prevention and crisis intervention organization for LGBTQ (lesbian, gay, bisexual, transgender, queer, and questioning) young people. Visit *thetrevorproject.org* or call *24/7/365 Lifeline at 866-4-U-TREVOR (866-488-7386)*

- Trans lifeline: Trans Lifeline is a trans-led organization that connects trans people to the community, support, and resources they need to survive and thrive. Visit *translifeline.org/* or call *(877) 565-8860*

- StopBullying.Gov: This website offers resources specifically for teens to prevent bullying in their schools and communities and provides resources for those being bullied. *stopbullying.gov*

- Teens Against Bullying: Created by and for teens, this website is a place for middle and high school students to find ways to address bullying, take action, be heard, and own an important social cause. *pacerteensagainstbullying.org*

- Al-Anon/Alateen: A place just for teens affected by someone else's alcoholism. Visit *al-anon.org/newcomers/teen-corner-alateen/*

- Teen line: Teen Line provides support, resources, and hope to young people through a hotline of professionally trained teen counselors, and outreach programs that de-stigmatize and normalize mental health. CALL *800-852-8336* or *TEXT TEEN to 839863*

APPS & TECH SERVICES

- **Beacon 2.0:** Beacon is a portal to online applications (websites, mobile applications, and internet support groups) for mental disorders reviewed and rated by health experts. *beacon.anu.edu.au/*

- **Health Talk:** This website reflects the lived experience of mental health conditions, including research-based modules with hours of recording and analysis. *healthtalk.org/peoples-experiences/mental-health*

- **Mindfulness for Teens:** This website has resources to help teens use mindfulness to handle stress and includes apps to practice meditation and guided mediation recordings. *mindfulnessforteens.com*

- **Strength of Us**: An online community designed to inspire young adults impacted by mental health issues to think positive, stay strong, and achieve goals through peer support and resource sharing. *strengthofus.org*

- **Calm:** App for Sleep, Meditation and Relaxation. The app includes guided meditations, Sleep Stories, breathing programs and relaxing music and more.

- **Pacifica:** Pacifica helps teens break the cycle of ongoing negative thoughts. It does this by using tools that target stress, anxiety, and depression. The app consists of psychologist-designed tools based on Cognitive Behavioral Therapy, mindfulness meditation, relaxation and mood/health tracking.

-**7 Cups: Online Therapy and Chat:** This app offers free, anonymous, emotional support and counseling from trained active listeners. There is a text chat feature and listeners are available 24/7. Teens can also share their thoughts with peers. Described as "emotional support on demand."

RESOURCES

- **Center for Young Women's Health and Young Men's Health:** These websites provide a series of guides on emotional health, including test anxiety, depression, bullying, and eating disorders. *youngwomenshealth.org* and *youngmenshealthsite.org*

- **Go Ask Alice!:** Geared at young adults, this question and answer website contains a large database of questions about a variety of concerns surrounding emotional health. *goaskalice.columbia.edu*

- **Girls Health.Gov:** The "Your Feelings" section of this website offers guidance to teenage girls on recognizing a mental health problem, getting help, and talking to parents. *girlshealth.gov/feelings*

- **Jed Foundation:** Promoting emotional health and preventing suicide among college students, this website provides an online resource center, ULifeline, a public dialogue forum, Half of Us, and Transition Year, resources and tools to help students transition to college. *jedfoundation.org/students*

- **Kelty Mental Health Resource Center:** Reference sheets are provided that list top websites, books, videos, toolkits, and support for mental health disorders. *keltymentalhealth.ca/youth-and-young-adults*

- **Teens Health:** Providing a safe place for teens who need honest and accurate information, this website provides resources on mental health issues. *teenshealth.org/teen/your_mind*

- **Teen Mental Health:** Geared towards teenagers, this website provides learning tools on a variety of mental illnesses, videos, and resources for friends. *teenmentalhealth.org*

- **Reach Out Recovery:** Get addiction recovery information and daily inspiration. Help to raise drug free kids, workbooks for the whole family and support. *Reachoutrecovery.com*

ROR DOCUMENTARIES
AVAILABLE AT: REACHOUTRECOVERY.COM/PRODUCTS

The Secret World Of Recovery
2016 ASAM Media Award winning documentary reveals life on the other side of addiction. Shown at film festivals, colleges, in recovery treatment centers, and community groups nationwide. 37 minutes, all audiences.

The Silent Majority
Teen prevention documentary showcases five programs that empower teens to make healthy lifestyle choices. First aired on PBS station WEDU 2014, The Silent Majority was distributed to PBS stations nationwide by American Public Television 2015. 48 minutes, all audiences

REACH OUT RECOVERY BOOKS

AVAILABLE AT: REACHOUTRECOVERY.COM/PRODUCTS

Find Your True Colors in 12 Steps
Expanded Edition
Incorporating recovery principles, self-expression,and the calming joy of coloring. For all ages and recovery programs.

100 Tips For Growing Up
My 20 Years of Recovery
By Lindsey Glass
A step-by-step adulting guide to becoming your best self after addiction. Compiled from 20 years of advice from the experts. This 150-page book includes tips, notes for action, and space for journaling. Ages 13+

My Family is Hurting What Can I Do
The 8 C's Coloring Book
By Leslie Glass, Illustrated by Jacob Cleveland
The delightful coloring book story of a child learning the 8 C's of reassurance and empowerment to help overcome adverse experiences. Comes with adult workbook Ages 6-10